# TERRY FOX

**Erratum**

In the first printing of *Terry Fox: His Story,* the captions for the photographs on page 150 were inadvertently reversed. The top photo is of Terry Fox receiving the Order of Canada from the Governor General; in the bottom photo the presentation is being made by Premier Bill Bennett.

Although this error has been corrected, it may be found in your copy. If it is, please accept our apologies.

Ah, but a man's reach should exceed his grasp,
Or what's a heaven for?

*Robert Browning, 1855*

# TERRY FOX

## HIS STORY

## by
## Leslie Scrivener

McCLELLAND AND STEWART

The Canadian Publishers
McClelland and Stewart Limited
25 Hollinger Road, Toronto M4B 3G2

CANADIAN CATALOGUING IN PUBLICATION DATA

Scrivener, Leslie, 1950-
  Terry Fox: his story

ISBN 0-7710-8017-4

I. Fox, Terry, 1958-  II. Cancer – Biography.
III. Runners (Sports) – Canada – Biography.
I. Title.

RC263.S37   616.99'471'0924   C81-094617-3

Manufactured in Canada by Webcom Limited

# Acknowledgements

My thanks to Terry and his family for their trust; to Bonnie Cornell, my editor at the *Toronto Star* for her foresight and enthusiasm; to Martin Goodman, president of the *Toronto Star*, for his support; to the staff of the Canadian Cancer Society both in Vancouver and Toronto, especially Dr. Robert Macbeth, Barbara Kilvert, Colleen Morris, Lynn Bryan, and Blair MacKenzie; to Terry's doctors, especially Dr. Michael Noble, for their patience and openness; to Tim Padmore and Chris Gainor of the *Vancouver Sun* for their insightful and National Newspaper Award winning medical series; to George Woodcock for his comment on heroism in *Canada and Canadians*; to Rika Noda; to Jennifer Glossop; and to Paul, my husband, for his good temper.

# Prologue

"The whole thing was such a romantic adventure and all of it was happening to *me*. People began calling me a hero, but as far as I was concerned, I was just simple little old Terry Fox. It was like Dorothy in *The Wizard of Oz*, going through this great big adventure, going places she had never been and seeing things she had never seen before and things happening that had never happened.

"I loved it. I enjoyed myself so much and that was what other people couldn't realize. They thought I was going through a nightmare running all day long. People thought I was going through hell. Maybe I was, partly, but still I was doing what I wanted and a dream was coming true and that, above everything else, made it all worthwhile to me. Even though it was so difficult, there was not another thing in the world I would rather have been doing.

"I got satisfaction out of doing things that were difficult. It was an incredible feeling. The pain was there, but the pain didn't matter. But that's all a lot of people could see; they couldn't see the good that I was getting out of it myself."

# Chapter One

They knew something of dreamers in St. John's. Living in Canada's most easterly city, they had seen a handful of young men with good muscle tone and high hopes promise to walk, run, or cycle from coast to coast, or even to row across the Atlantic for a worthy cause. Not that the people of St. John's – North America's oldest city – were cynical. It was just that they had seen it all before – a little fanfare and the fellow disappeared down the road or out to sea.

But on April 12, 1980, a bitter rainy morning – when, as they said in Newfoundland, winter was still abounding – there was an extra flutter of excitement in the town. Another runner was about to set out, but this one caused more of a buzz than his predecessors. Her worship, Mayor Dorothy Wyatt, was interested in him and so was the CBC.

His name, they heard, was Terry Fox, and he was getting ready over at the Holiday Inn. In fact, he was on the floor in his room doing thirty-five push-ups and sixty sit-ups. That wasn't unusual for a twenty-one-year-old, except that this one, better looking than most with a well-scrubbed, intelligent face, straight teeth, and an Adonis-like profile – which would make older women feel maternal and teenagers feverish – had only one leg. His right leg was a stump, amputated six inches above the knee, and it was attached to a prosthesis, an artificial limb made of fibreglass and steel. His left leg was taut and muscular.

He pulled on a pair of jeans, a Ford of Canada T-shirt, and a ski jacket, and went downstairs for breakfast. He could order whatever he wanted – both the room and the meals were on the house. That made him smile. It was thoughtful and showed that people

7

weren't writing him off as a kook. After all, a one-legged runner who dreamed of crossing Canada – it could have been a bad joke. Most cross-country runners preferred to take advantage of the westerly winds by starting in Vancouver and running to Halifax, a journey 900 miles shorter than the one Terry dreamed of completing.

In the hotel restaurant, he ordered carbohydrates with enthusiasm. Let them laugh at his French toast, his side order of hash browns, and the couple of muffins. He knew they were energy food; the calories served their purpose.

Terry was accompanied by an old schoolfriend, Doug Alward. Shy, soft-spoken, and bedrock stubborn, Doug was a small man, the same age as Terry, with thin, dark hair that was receding prematurely, glasses, and a perpetually quizzical look. Together, they left the hotel to look at their brand-new camper van, donated by Ford of Canada and outfitted by Funcraft. A traveller's dream, it had air conditioning, a stove, fridge, washroom, stereo, and could accommodate six. On the side was printed MARATHON OF HOPE CROSS COUNTRY RUN IN AID OF CANCER RESEARCH.

Terry and Doug started loading the van with the boxes of cereal, oranges, chocolate-chip cookies, bags of chips and Cheezies, boxes of doughnuts, tins of stew and spaghetti, and, of course, peanut butter and jelly. This is it, Terry was thinking. This is really it. I'm going to start running.

Later, Donna Green, a girl Terry had met at the Newfoundland Summer Games, stopped by to give him a good-luck card and a pennant. Terry, who had wanted to collect mementos of his trip, realized that pennants from every town along the way would mark his route perfectly.

He napped for a while until Bill Strong, field supervisor for the Canadian Cancer Society, which endorsed and promised to publicize his run, stopped by to take him for a drive, while Doug bought gas for the van. Bill remembered that Terry had wanted to collect two gallons of Atlantic seawater, which he planned to carry in the van to the Pacific Ocean – one he would empty at the end of his 5,300-mile run, the other he would keep as a souvenir. Bill reasoned if Terry was going to all that effort he might as well have clear water, rather than the murky stuff that swilled along the city wharf.

They drove to the outskirts of the city where the bald and rocky shore met the sea. It was a dour, dull day. The rain had stopped, but clouds and mist hugged the hills. The cove was deserted.

Bill gallantly volunteered to fill the jugs. He had just perched on what he thought was a safe rock when a wave of cold Atlantic seawater crashed on the shore and soaked his three-piece suit. "I was distraught," Bill explained later. He was so distraught he dropped the gallon jug and watched unhappily as it floated out to sea. Terry hooted with laughter and offered to try himself. As Bill snapped away with his camera, Terry walked up from the beach holding a jug, barely half full.

That was Terry's private ceremony. The next was for the public at the foot of Temperance Street near St. John's harbour. This time he wore shorts and a T-shirt. The beach was muddy, littered with construction from a sewage tunnel. There were bulldozers in the background and guy wires covered with seaweed. It wasn't the prettiest place to start, Terry said, but it was the beginning.

Terry turned his back to the sea and clasped his arms behind him in the position every high-school basketball player assumes when his photo is being taken for the yearbook. Back straight, eyes forward. The CBC television cameras whirred and Bill's camera clicked, sea gulls squawked and Terry dipped his artificial leg in the water and bent down to touch the pebbles. A run didn't count in his mind unless he touched something.

He set off up a gravel hill with newsmen and a handful of spectators beside him. He told the reporters he wanted to raise one million dollars and hoped to run thirty to forty miles a day to get home to Port Coquitlam, near Vancouver, within six months. He even planned to run across Vancouver Island to Port Renfrew so he could dip his leg in the Pacific. His run, like Canada's motto, would be from sea to sea.

A reporter remarked that he sounded pretty confident.

"If it's only up to me and my mind," Terry said, "I've got a lot of positive attitude. I think I can do it. But you never know what might happen."

He left the reporters behind and started running through the old, tired part of St. John's, past boarded-up shops, tumbled-down marinas with signs offering cold beer, along the empty sidewalks. Occasionally, people would turn to watch, and their faces would show shock or grimaces of surprise. Their thoughts were transparent: Good God, he's running with only one leg. How can he do it?

Terry gave them a wave and continued up the broad ramp leading to St. John's showy, slate-grey city hall. Her worship, Mayor Wyatt herself welcomed him. She was wearing dark glasses, a startling polka-dot pantsuit and her robes of office. She clasped Terry to her as though he were her son, dropped her chain of office over his T-shirt, and hung on his arm as he signed her guest book. The book rested on a wooden podium carved with the Lamb of St. John the Baptist. The room was fragrant with Easter lilies. Terry smiled into Bill's camera and kept thinking, This is really it.

Then Mrs. Wyatt draped her red and gold robe over Terry's shoulders and led him out to the concrete terrace to talk to the crowd outside. He was nervous and worried about what he would say. He also worried that he looked a little goofy with his running shorts sticking out from beneath the mayor's robe. Mayor Wyatt presented him with messages for the mayors of Vancouver and Victoria and a little flag for him which he twirled nervously in his palm. Then she ordered that the Canadian Cancer Society flag be raised. In her speech to the crowd – they seemed chilly and kept their hands in their parka pockets – she spoke of the great challenge that lay before Terry.

Then he made his first speech. He challenged the people of Newfoundland to match his running effort by donating money. He told them he lost his leg to cancer.

Mrs. Wyatt took the stand again and again ordered that the Cancer Society flag be raised. It was already up. Terry grinned. The crowd grinned. The irrepressible mayor grinned, and Terry returned her robe and chain.

He started running: taking a double hop with the left leg and one long step with his metal leg. Someone called it the Fox Trot. His hands were clenched. He leaned forward for more speed. Looks of disbelief crossed the faces of the hundred or so onlookers. Then they gave a little cheer and clapped. A police cruiser, its lights flashing, drove beside Terry. Mrs. Wyatt set off enthusiastically behind, her robe flapping. She couldn't keep up and followed in her car.

Terry ran out on the highway past the brownish hills dotted

with patches of snow. The fishing boats and moorage wharfs were far behind, but the mayor wasn't. She caught up in her car, leapt out of her red robe and skipped along behind him, her chain of office beating on her pantsuit as she ran. It was wacky and wonderful and Terry was delighted. He'd never forget any of it.

A mile or so out of St. John's, Terry realized his sock was wet, probably the result of his gamboling for seawater. He stopped to ask Doug to find a dry one. It was already mid-afternoon and Terry was anxious to get the miles behind him.

Doug hadn't had time to get the van in order and found it difficult to find a sock quickly beneath the bags of groceries. Terry was impatient. After all, he'd had a terrific send-off, and now he was forced to stand on the highway and ask for a sock.

"I could tell," Doug said later a little mournfully, "that our troubles had already started."

All that afternoon, passing cars honked their horns, and Terry delighted in the friendly waves from the drivers. Doug kept the van in front of him, driving one mile ahead and waiting until Terry caught up. Terry thought a lot as he ran. He imagined the road would be lonely for the next six months, but he was used to that. He thought about Stanley Park in Vancouver, where he would run his last mile. He'd be the happiest man in Canada.

He felt the cold. He was used to that, too. He could run in rain, bitter wind; and he could run uphill and down; he could run a hundred days in a row without taking a break. His body was a running machine, and his mind was the force behind it.

Terry wasn't tormented by angst, self-doubt, depression, or any other twentieth-century anxiety. He was brimming with determination and hope. He was a dreamer, although the enormity of his vision didn't frighten him even as he pounded out those first miles. "Who would have thought it would be possible to run across Canada on one leg, eh?" he said. "I wanted to try the impossible and show that it could be done. I've always been competitive and I wanted to show myself, and other people, too, that I could do it. To show them that I wasn't disabled or handicapped."

He knew, too, that he was an ordinary guy, what his mother called average in everything but determination. He was, in fact, a garden-variety Canadian who adored hockey stars Bobby Orr and Darryl Sittler, respected the Maple Leaf, liked to watch pretty girls walk by, enjoyed inspirational poetry, had never heard of, let alone read, *War and Peace*, was touched by the affection of children, believed in national unity, and wondered why the heck Quebec wanted to separate anyway.

He ran twelve and a half miles that first day before he was stopped by darkness and the cold fog that had crept down from the hills. The Marathon of Hope had been invited back to the Holiday Inn to sleep. They accepted rather than spend the night in the topsy-turvy van. Besides, the propane heater wasn't working, and they knew it would be a cold night. In his motel room, Terry took out his diary, a big, ledger-sized book, and wrote: *Today is the day it all begins* and filled a page with details of his day. Then he fell asleep, contented.

As he slept, his parents were awake on the other side of the country, tuned to the CBC national news. They watched, in considerable amazement, the auspicious beginning of their son's dream.

The next day Terry began to understand the audacity of that dream and the punishing price of achievement. He got up at 4:30 the next morning and ran until 9 A.M. when he stopped for a breakfast of grapefruit and cereal. When he started running later in the day he was buffeted by forty-mile-an-hour winds, which tore through the light jacket and three layers of shirts he wore. He told his diary, *It knocked me off the road and almost on my butt.* The sores on his stump started hurting. His heart began to flutter dangerously. He rested, wrapped in a blanket. By mid-afternoon, he had completed what he had thought would be impossible – twenty miles. It was the toughest twenty miles he had ever run but, always striving to do better, he told himself if it hadn't been for the wind whipping across the frozen lakes onto the highway, he'd have done thirty miles.

When Terry turned off the light in the lower bunk of the van that night, he knew the next day would be no easier. The forecast called for snow. By breakfast he was running in a blizzard and slipping on the icy road; by lunch the wind held him to a standstill, yet he managed sixteen miles.

They parked the van that night in a schoolyard and slept in it until a Royal Canadian Mounted Police constable knocked on the door and offered them a motel room.

The next day Doug started accepting donations through the van window as he waited for Terry at each mile marker. One driver pulled up and pushed fifty dollars through the window. "I don't care if he makes it," he told Doug. "He's really making a lot of people feel good."

They stopped that night at a store in Bellevue and were invited in by the Brazil family for a shower and a meal. Doug noticed that someone had clipped Terry's picture out of a newspaper and thought enough of him to tack it up above the dining-room table.

Terry treasured it all. He stored every memory. Every cheer – the one he heard most often was pure Newfoundland: "You sure got the nerve" – every kind word, every offer of a meal helped him run another mile, helped ease the aches and the irritations and convinced him his dream was not a mere foolishness. The ordinary Canadians tucked away in those tiny seaside towns cared about him. He felt it. His enthusiasm soared.

People heard his message: a disability didn't have to be a handicap. Cancer could be beaten. As the dollars poured in the van window, Terry saw, much to his own amazement, that he was inspiring others while being inspired himself.

"Knowing that there are people who care about what I'm doing, that I'm not just running across Canada, that there are people who are giving money to help fight the disease that took my leg and to help other people who are lying down in hospital beds all over the world, it's a reward."

# Chapter Two

His parents were Betty and Rolly Fox. When Terry started his run, Betty was forty-two. She had prematurely grey hair, which framed her head in tight curls. Her smile was pretty, and when it flashed you knew it was the real thing. When she was irritated, however, it was better to be out of the room. She was blunt, some might think to the point of harshness. When it came to protecting her children, Terry in particular, Betty was like a mother lion. She could snap fiercely or be moved to tears more quickly than most people.

Terry respected her judgement and agreed with most of her decisions. As he was running, businessmen would ask if Terry would endorse their product – one asked merely that Terry drive away in his vehicle when the run was over. His mother handled all such requests, and in Terry's eyes, she was doing a darn good job. It was as though they had one mind. She was proud to say, as she often did, "I know Terry better than anyone." In time, when the world started wanting too big a piece of her son, she became possessive and protective and defied the world to call her what it wanted. She was doing what was best for Terry.

Rolly was forty-five when Terry started his run. He was a Canadian National Railway switchman, and had been since 1954. His hair was reddish brown, his complexion ruddy, and his temperament, to those who knew him just a little, seemed quiet, though his family always said he harboured a quick and stubborn temper. There was generosity in his spirit, and he always made an effort to make one feel at ease. Despite his reticence, he warmed to strangers more quickly than Betty did. Although it seemed he often deferred to his wife, who eventually became the family spokesman, they were a team.

They were both salt of the earth and dependable, and their family came first in their lives. Their children were close to them without being dependent. It was a fine line, and they walked it expertly. They didn't go in for frills – both wore jeans as much as anything else – and they lived in a comfortable suburban home about seventeen miles east of Vancouver. In the living room there was a pair of carved moose on the fireplace mantel, and the fancy velvet pillows were still protected under plastic wrap. When they finally finished their basement, they put in a pool table.

Betty and Rolly met in Winnipeg. Betty, a former tomboy who could throw a ball with the best of her brothers, had escaped the little farming town of Melita to study hair-dressing in the big city. Neither she nor Rolly finished high school. They married in 1956.

Betty was so practical that when the labour pains started with her first child and there was no car to take her to the hospital, she simply packed her bags and walked.

Their first son was named Fred, after her brother. The family would have its first taste of tragedy when the elder Fred lost both his legs in a plane crash during a whiteout in northern Manitoba. The next taste came a few years later when Betty's youngest sister, Norma, who lived with them, was killed when her car skidded into a tanker on black ice on the Lougheed Highway. The family wondered if somehow they had been unfairly singled out.

Terrance Stanley arrived July 28, 1958, and was named after uncles on both sides of the family. Darrell was born in 1962, followed two years later by Judith. The family was complete.

Betty's only significant memories of Terry as an infant were that he loved to chew on sticks and was a slow walker. The early pictures of him, kept in the big box of old photographs, show a somewhat serious-looking child, wearing a good white shirt and bow tie in one photo, a cowboy shirt with fringed trousers in another. Despite the exterior calm he displayed for the cameraman, internally Terry was cultivating a character that lasted into adulthood. Its most prominent characteristic was tenacity, a quality he applied even to his building blocks. Betty recalled that as a toddler he stacked wooden blocks relentlessly. If they refused to stay up there where he put them, he became frustrated and furious. He stacked them again and again until he was successful.

That mulishness ran in the family. When Betty gave up smoking, a lot of her friends told her she'd just start again. The taunt was like a challenge. She never gave anyone the satisfaction of saying I told you so. Terry had the same nature.

He cultivated patience, too. As a child he loved games that lasted for days. Luckily, he enjoyed his own company because few children had his perseverance even in play. He played contentedly by himself for hours.

Sometimes he set up the portable hockey game and devised a long, complicated season's schedule. He would play for both teams, allowing three passes before he would switch sides and shoot for the other team. He continued playing long after his interest in working the players had waned, he said, because he wanted to see who won. Also, as his father had taught him, he liked to finish what he started.

Terry loved playing soldiers, too. He would bundle up carpets and make fortresses of them in the basement, arranging his armies of cowboys and Indians or soldiers from both world wars on either side. When the soldiers lay face down, they were dead; face up, they were wounded. He fought to the last man.

By 1966 Rolly wanted a change from the harsh Manitoba winters and transferred to Surrey (at the price of twelve years' seniority). Two years later, he moved the family to Port Coquitlam.

The boys all loved sports, whether it was road hockey or baseball, and they all liked to win. Sometimes Terry and Fred would gang up on Rolly as he lay on the chesterfield. They would pummel him, and he'd fight the pair of them. Everyone did his best to get in the last lick, although Fred and Terry would usually be in tears before the rough-housing was over. "We really fought dirty," Terry remembered. "We'd be bawling our eyes out but we'd come back for more. Even to get one more shot in was worth it."

Since Rolly frequently worked the afternoon shift, it was often Betty who, reviving her tomboy instincts, threw a ball in the backyard with her sons. When Terry learned how to pitch a baseball, Betty was there playing catcher.

After work, Betty and Rolly watched their sons compete in soccer games. Often all three boys were playing in their own age groups on three different soccer fields in the same day.

Discipline in the Fox household was strict. Betty may have made more noise than her quiet husband, but he was the one who enforced order and made sure the rules were obeyed. Betty and Rolly had a basic code of values for their children – don't get in trouble with the law; don't take drugs; when you get a job, keep it. The children started working early by berry picking when they were nine and ten years old. They continued at the seasonal jobs when they were teenagers. By twelve or thirteen, they were buying their own school clothing and later would buy their own golf clubs and ten-speed bikes. "Everything wasn't handed to them, they all had to learn to do for themselves," Betty said, although she would never allow her children to take a paper route because she felt it wasn't fair for kids to get up at 5 A.M. Occasional jobs were fine for children, but they needed their rest and they needed their free time.

Terry loved sports and participated eagerly, even in elementary school where he played baseball. Sometimes he'd arrive at the corner where he was to pick up his ride to the game an hour early, just to make sure he'd get there on time. Then, after kicking the curb for half an hour, waiting, not very patiently, he'd think he missed the ride and agonize the next half hour away until the car turned up.

By grade eight, Terry and his friend Doug Alward had come to the attention of Bob McGill, their physical education teacher at Mary Hill Junior High School.

Bob remembered Terry as "the little guy who worked his rear off. If there was a race, he'd be in the middle of the pack. In class, he'd be sitting three-quarters of the way back, so small that in the big junior-high desks his feet wouldn't touch the floor. His head would be lowered, and if a teacher was looking for answers to questions, Terry would be saying to himself, 'Oh, God, please don't let him ask me, please. If he does, I'll just die.' And if a girl happened to look his way, he'd just shy away."

Doug was much the same. He and Terry had at least three things in common in grade eight: both were introverts; both measured exactly five feet tall, and both loved basketball. There was one difference, however. Doug, who was also a talented cross-country runner, was a first-string basketball player, whereas Terry was simply terrible at the game, even by the standards of the Mary Hill Cobras.

Bob suggested Terry try out for cross-country running. He might as well have asked Terry to sky dive; the boy had no interest in running. Terry started the rigorous training anyway, because he had so much respect for the coach and wanted to please him.

Terry found the cross-country workouts exhausting, and he was often afraid to start the runs because the pace was so demanding. The biggest reward came at the end of the run, when the coach would welcome the runners in, and say, "Well done, *men.*" That's what Terry remembered: his teacher congratulating the skinny young boys on their efforts by calling them men.

Terry still wanted to play basketball. After three basketball practices, Bob McGill suggested kindly that he might be better suited for wrestling. Bob had noticed other small boys who showed more ability as guards. But Terry was determined to stick with the game, even if he was the nineteenth player on a team of nineteen. He worked hard in practice and was rewarded with one minute of floor play all season. He thought his team mates laughed at him for that, but he didn't let it get him down.

That summer he decided to show them. They wouldn't laugh at him next year. He called Doug and said, "Do you want to play a little one-on-one?" Doug, at the other end of the line, paused, remembering that Terry was a pretty fair runner, but a dreadful basketball player, and said no.

But, like a bulldog, Terry persisted. The second time he called, Doug agreed. "I could probably beat him twenty-one to nothing, but I don't remember if I ever did. He might get ten points off me," Doug said, "but the point was he couldn't beat me."

The two boys played hard all summer. Doug's older brother Jack, who was a gifted high-school basketball player, often joined them, coaching and playing. By grade nine, there were four boys regularly pounding the floor of the Mary Hill gym every morning before school. Doug wasn't one of them, but Terry was.

"Mom and Dad didn't like me getting up early to go to school to play basketball," Terry recalled. "Because they didn't want me to go early, I'd wait until the very last minute to get out of bed. I'd eat my breakfast as fast as I could, and I'd run all the way – and

Mary Hill was far from our house. I'd run in the dark with all my books and clothes flying."

He remembered days when he felt sick with flu or a cold, days when he should have stayed in bed, but on those days he forced himself to his feet and ran to school anyway. He didn't want to fall behind in his classwork, but most of all he didn't want to miss a moment of basketball.

Bob McGill had that effect on all the boys on the team. When he said, "If you want something, you work for it, because I'm not interested in mediocrity," Terry and the others listened. Bob told them they could be the best but only if they got up early, practised before school, and stayed late afterwards. Terry responded to his teacher as though the man were a Norman Vincent Peale in running shoes. He didn't call him Mr. McGill as the other boys did. He called him Coach; he said it with respect.

McGill's policy was not to cut anyone from the team, but he let the boys know that only the twelve best players would be allowed floor time. In grade nine, Terry was one of the twelve best. He wanted to be as good as the coach said he could be. He wanted to please him. "He was such an inspirational type person, I wanted to show him that I was a lot better than being laughed at by the other players," Terry recalled.

McGill chuckled with pride, remembering the way he drove them all and the way Terry, in particular, responded: "If I had told Terry to hit his head against the wall, he would have," Bob said. "Because that's how much he believed in what I was trying to do."

By grade ten, Terry had earned a spot as a starting guard. His pal Doug was one of the co-winners of the Athlete of the Year Award at Mary Hill. They'd both earned respect, too. Bob McGill remembered Doug and Terry starting against the tallest team in their league. When the Johnston Heights boys lined up against the Mary Hill boys, they just started laughing. Doug and Terry may have sprouted to five feet six inches, but the boys they had to check measured in at five feet eleven inches and six feet one inch.

There's no question who won, but at the end of the game, the two Johnston Heights guards came over to shake hands with Doug and Terry. They knew they'd been in a game.

In grade eleven, when Terry joined the Port Coquitlam High

School Ravens basketball team, he was a starting guard. Doug, who had taken a term at Centennial High School because it offered a better athletic program, remembered Terry once scored twenty points in the first half of a game. "All of a sudden, he'd become somebody by working hard," Doug said. Even when the team was being clobbered, the basketball coach, Terri Fleming, recalled that Terry never gave up.

By 1976, the one-on-one games between Terry and Doug were repeated but with a new twist: Terry could now beat Doug twenty-one to nothing. Except once. Doug recalled: "Terry was taller than me in grade twelve, and I remember playing with him in practice. I faked him out, and to my horror, I scored on him. I couldn't believe I had scored. He was mad, and the reason he was mad was that he had let down. He had thought, 'Ah, Alward, I can stuff him,' but I had faked him out. He picked up the basketball and slammed it down hard on the floor. The other guys in the line-up just looked in stunned silence."

Terry was a good, all-round, reliable player, good enough to share the Athlete of the Year Award in grade twelve with Doug, who came second in British Columbia cross-country finals. Doug modestly claimed that Terry deserved the award more than he did because Terry was a better basketball player, a first-class soccer player, and a gutsy rugby player. Doug recalled one rugby game in particular: "This big guy got by everybody, and Terry was the last guy to stop him. Terry got him with this fantastic tackle. Man, he was tough! I could feel it from the sidelines. Holy cow, he should have had pads on. He may have been scared, but he'd stand there and face it."

Although Terry remembers being an average student at Mary Hill, the truth is he and Doug actually scrambled on to the honour roll a few times. Both share a nostalgia for biology. According to Doug, that science was made for them because it required lots of memorization. The two hard-driving athletes, who were by this time used to putting in long hours in training, applied the same discipline to memorizing a hundred pages of biology notes.

The competitive spirit they shared in sports was also transferred to their academic work. Doug, who seems to have been the sly one of the pair, turned to subterfuge to set Terry up again. This time his ploy was to tell Terry that he was not going to open a book to study for their next exam, but secretly, at home on the other side of town, Doug drove himself to desperation with study. When the exam results were posted, Terry was amazed to see that Doug had earned one of the top scores.

Later, analyzing the outcomes, Doug thought he beat Terry – who, he believed, was more naturally gifted – because Terry let down his guard. In his mind the challenge was diminished. And why did Doug act out the farce? "I wanted to beat him."

It was a competitive world Terry lived in.

Betty was annoyed when Terry belittled his academic abilities. She wasn't a pushy mother, but she let him know she had high expectations of him – such as medical or pharmacy school. Terry remembered presenting his mother with his school report card and watching her carefully, wondering what she thought of his grades. Were they good enough? Was she proud of him? Was he doing well? "Sometimes, because I knew she cared, I'd do things for her," he'd say. "Even in school I wanted to get good grades to show her I could do it." In the same vein, he was thrilled when his parents came to watch him play, and he still wondered if they thought he was good enough.

No doubt, Terry was eager to please people, especially those he respected, like Bob McGill and his parents. His achievements in school and sports were as much for their approval as for his own satisfaction.

Terry's interests and friendships broadened in high school. He went to basketball parties, would have couple of drinks with his buddies, and even got roaring drunk a couple of times. Doug, however, found it more difficult to break out of his shyness, and the two drifted apart.

Terry even started dating occasionally. "There were lots of girls I knew who liked me and wanted to go out with me, but I was still too shy," he said. He still didn't have a steady girlfriend. He felt more at ease with his locker-room friends, and his idea of a good time was a night playing basketball. Dinner dates and flowers would come later. Running with jocks, Terry stayed completely away from the drug culture that left some in his generation dozing on the beaches. He never sampled marijuana, even out of curiosity.

He graduated from Port Coquitlam High School with straight A's but for one B in English. Memorization and all the self-discipline in the world couldn't get him through essay writing, the subtleties of *Waiting for Godot*, and other high-school literary fare.

While Terry wasn't sure he wanted to go to university, Betty was sure he should. He went, partly to please her, partly to please himself.

He knew he wanted to play more basketball, though he realized the competition at university, especially at Simon Fraser – which had the best varsity team in British Columbia – would be fierce. Naturally, that was no deterrent to Terry.

He was also inclined to a career as a physical-education teacher in a high school. He liked the idea of being "the coach" to a bunch of skinny kids with more drive than ability. Since he enjoyed sports, he chose kinesiology, the study of human movement, as a major, although Betty would have preferred one of the professions.

It didn't surprise any of his former coaches or present friends that Terry tried out for the SFU junior varsity team. The two-week training camp run by basketball coach Alex Devlin was tough, more of an endurance test than anything else. Devlin and the players, including Mike McNeill, who now is the head basketball coach at SFU, saw others who were more gifted than Terry, but they saw none with more desire. McNeill, who was a first string guard on the varsity team at the time, remembered: "In the summer after high school we knew Terry was coming out for the team. I played against him offensively, and he wasn't that good, but defensively he was one of the toughest I've ever played against. He had a lot of pride and he worked hard."

During the training camp, Terry remembered Alex Devlin coming up to him and saying, "We've been noticing you."

Terry had made the team.

"There were more talented players who didn't make it," McNeill recalled, "but Terry just out-gutted them. People tend to look in awe at players who have a lot of natural ability, but respect from other athletes goes to the guy who works really hard." That was Terry.

For Terry, the physical discipline was one thing, but what ensured his success was his mental attitude, or as he called it, his mental toughness. He had learned that toughness partly from training in junior high school as a cross-country runner, partly in those long hours of playing one-on-one with whomever would have the patience to play with him, partly on the rugby field, where his opponents were pleased to trample him into the mud.

He had also learned it at home, where the friendly fisticuffs on the chesterfield were replaced with angry, sometimes lively, always bull-headed debate over cards, over who was the best player in the National Hockey League, over anything. Terry liked to be right. In fact, even when he was wrong he'd plug away in an argument until, by sheer will or intimidation, his brother or father would give up. Unfortunately, in the Fox household, almost everyone shared that attitude: "Stick up for yourself even if you're wrong." Argument didn't get him very far, but it seemed to entrench his stubborn will.

# Chapter Three

Terry would be the first to admit he was a dreamer. On November 12, 1976, he dreamed his 1968 green Cortina right into the back of a half-ton truck on the Lougheed Highway. He'd been watching construction of a new bridge over the Coquitlam River near the turn-off to his neighbourhood. Police arrived and Terry's car was towed away, never to be driven again. Terry walked away from the accident without a scratch. His right knee was a little sore, and he guessed he must have rammed it on the underside of the dashboard. He phoned his mother at the card shop where she worked, then hopped a bus to SFU and basketball practice.

In December, Terry noticed again a pain in that same knee. Many athletes have knee and ankle problems; aches are expected. Terry thought his ache was a result of playing so much basketball on the hard gym floor. He thought it might have been a cartilage problem, but whatever it was, it would have to stay away until the end of the basketball season. He didn't mention it to his coach or his parents.

A week after the season ended, in the last week of February, Terry finally went to the university medical services and was told he had a chemical reaction – he was not told to what – in his knee and was given a handful of pills. He took the pills for five days and believed they had worked because he didn't feel the pain any more. He didn't know they were pain killers.

One day at the beginning of March, Betty was home from work after an operation to remove a cyst from her foot. She looked out her living-room window and saw something terribly wrong. Terry, who had just run seven laps around the track at Hastings Junior High School, was limping slowly home. Betty slid down the front stairs to the door to help her son. She could barely stand up herself, but she grabbed him. The pain in his knee, he said, was unbearable.

She suggested a hot bath, the universal restorative, but rather than soothe his temper and pain, both were exacerbated. Terry could barely move and stumbled to bed.

The next day the knee was swollen and throbbing. Terry went to see a family doctor who was filling in for their own physician Robert Heffelfinger. He suspected a significant problem, possibly even cancer, and referred Terry to a bone specialist.

On March 3, when Terry woke up, he tried to stand and couldn't. Since he hadn't been able to get a quick appointment with a specialist, Betty lent Terry her crutches, and Rolly drove him to the emergency room at the Royal Columbian Hospital in New Westminster. She waited by the phone.

Twenty minutes after Dr. Michael Piper, an orthopedic specialist on duty in the hospital's plaster room, saw Terry, he knew he wasn't dealing with water on the knee or a cartilage problem. After looking at the shadows on the X-rays, he was pretty sure Terry had osteogenic sarcoma, a rare, malignant tumour that appears to develop more often in males then females and is most common among children and young adults aged ten to twenty-five. Sarcomas are tumours of the connective and supportive tissues of the body. Piper had only seen two tumours of that type in his practice.

Osteogenic sarcoma is the most common primary cancer of the bone. It is a destroyer that usually begins its work near the knee and makes the bone soft and mushy so that the grain that streaks the bone looks like a highway that ends abruptly in a swamp. As the sarcoma grows, it breaks through the bone into surrounding muscles and tendons. Unlike lung cancer, which can be linked to environmental hazards such as smoking, no one knows what causes osteogenic sarcoma. Terry believed his car accident caused a weakness in his knee and made him susceptible to a tumour. His doctors, however, said there was no connection.

Although the sarcoma was rare, it was well known. Its victims have included Edward Kennedy, Jr. (son of the U.S. senator), who lost his leg in 1973.

If Piper's diagnosis was confirmed by further testing, including a bone scan, there would be no time to waste. Treatment was surgery, and it had to be done as soon as possible. As soon as the malignant tumour develops, its cells start to multiply, and the body's immunity systems cannot stand the attack by the aberrant cells. The tumour sends cells, like invasion forces, into the blood stream to be carried all over the body.

Terry, however, learned none of this that morning. The doctor took Rolly aside to say he believed Terry had a malignant tumour but he did not want the boy to be told until he had a second opinion. He suggested that Rolly take Terry out for breakfast and then bring him back to the hospital later, when a room would be available. In the meantime, Dr. Piper consulted with the two senior surgeons. He asked one of them if he would take the patient. Piper, who is orthopedic surgeon for the Vancouver Canucks hockey team, had been in practice three years and thought of orthopedics as a happy speciality, a practice of healing and mending, not of amputating. He would, however, stay on the case, break the news to Terry, and perform the amputation.

Meanwhile, Rolly walked immediately to a phone booth to call Betty. As he was telling the news to her, he broke down and cried. He knew he would have to face Terry a few minutes later so he gathered himself, tried to wipe the strain from his face, and took Terry to McDonald's. The bitterness Rolly still feels started growing that morning.

Terry was puzzled that day. He hadn't been told anything and he didn't know why. If he had to go back to the hospital for more examinations – a bone scan, blood tests, a chest X-ray – it must be something pretty serious; in fact, it might be something horrible. To him, horrible was a very bad cartilage or ligament problem. He started fantasizing about what might happen: would they cut out part of his leg, or, the worst nightmare, would they cut off all of his leg?

While Terry had breakfast, a call was made to Judith Ray, head nurse on the children's orthopedic ward, asking if an eighteen-year-old boy with possible ostengenic sarcoma could have a room in her ward. He had been admitted to hospital but there was no room for him on the adult ward. Would she accept him? She immediately said yes and told her staff. Several objected to an older patient, but Judith explained to them her feeling that the children's ward would be a better place for Terry because when a person is sick, he needs to regress a little bit and become a little more childlike. "It's really hard when you're an older teenager and so many people are telling you to behave like a man, and you really wish you were just a kid again," said Judith.

After she greeted Terry, Rolly, and Betty, who had joined them, at the elevator, she asked him what he'd been told. He said his right knee hurt, and he was waiting for the results of tests. She could tell from the strain on his parents' faces they probably already knew what the diagnosis was. She could tell by Terry's expression that he hadn't been told. Judith was disturbed. She couldn't understand why an eighteen-year-old couldn't be told of his probable condition while his parents could and were forced to keep a stiff upper lip. She knew he had to be told as quickly as possible.

He was given a bed in a ward with eight other boys. Judith looked on it as a summer camp with children of all ages. She thought it would be good for Terry. It was more like a home than a hospital, and he might look on the younger boys as kid brothers. Besides, he was likely to find someone in worse shape than himself on the ward, and with so much activity there wasn't time for brooding or self-pity. Judith convinced his parents that the ward was better for Terry than a private room.

March 4. Judith took Terry for a bone scan, the major test to determine his diagnosis. A technician gave him an injection of a radioactive material with an affinity for bone tissue, then looked at a screen to see where the substance localized. The tumour appeared as a hot spot on the screen. The diagnosis was immediately clear to the technician, and he made a sign to Judith – it was cancer.

On his way out in a wheelchair, Terry cheerfully said, "Thank you very much," to the technician.

"Don't thank me," he replied.

"Why did he say that?" Terry asked Judith.

Thinking fast, she said, "Oh, most people don't thank you for sticking needles into them."

Since bad news wasn't delivered in a nine-bed ward, Betty, Rolly, Judith, and Darrell were taken with Terry into a little room off the admitting area. Betty caught Judith's eye, wondering if the younger children should listen. "You're all part of the family and you've got to share things," the nurse told them.

"I knew there was something wrong, oh boy, did I know,"

Terry remembered, "when the whole family came in and Mom put her arm around me. The doctor came in and just told me, 'You've got a malignant tumour.' I guess I was supposed to be upset. I didn't do anything. 'What's that?' I said."

Piper told him he had a type of cancer, that his leg would have to be amputated soon, that he would undergo a series of chemotherapy treatments because there might be cancer cells circulating in his blood, and that he was going to lose his hair. The doctor said because of advances in research, new drugs had been developed to give him a 50- to 70-per-cent chance of survival. Two years earlier, his chances would have been about 15 per cent. Terry became an inmmediate believer in the value of traditional cancer research.

The doctor also told Terry, because he would hear about it sooner or later, about a fifteen-year-old girl from Port Coquitlam who had gone to the same high school as Terry. She'd had the same type of tumour and had been cared for in the same ward. Terry asked what happened to her and was told she had died that summer.

And Terry said: "Oh, fuck, I'm not ready to leave this world."

Rolly forgot about the ache in his heart; the tragedy of cancer was pushed aside while his brain registered shock. Like most strict parents, he had never heard his son swear before.

Then came the tears. Terry dropped his head on his chest. His family werit to him and they all wept together. Darrell, who was fifteen at :he time, remembered he and little Judith "bawled our eyes out.' Terry, seeing this, turned to comfort his younger brother and sister.

The Foxes may have been critical and competitive, but more than anything they were a strong, unified family who had known tragedy and loss before. They could handle this one, too. But Betty couldn't help wondering to herself: Is there a God? Think of all the things He's dealt our family over the years.

Doug Alward was there, too, waiting out in the hallway. Rolly called him in. "There was dead silence," he remembered. "It seemed as if no one knew what to say. I think Terry was crying and somehow I felt out of place."

After Dr. Piper left, Judith Ray dried her tears and set to work. "All right," she told Terry, "the news is crummy, but you can either mope or you can fight it." She suspected he was a fighter anyway. She told him many amputees played sports and even went skiing. She asked him what other sports he enjoyed. Judith was already working on Terry's healing. When he asked her about school – he had six weeks left in his semester – she teased him, the beginning of a bantering rapport that the two established later, and said, "What are you trying to do? Get out of school? No way." She explained he could do his school work with the help of a tutor while he learned to walk. Making arrangements with Simon Fraser University would give his parents something to do as well, and organizing Terry's classmates to tape his lectures would keep Doug busy.

After that night Terry never looked back. His world was turned around, but he decided to look on the loss of his leg as a new challenge. He was going to work hard, just as he worked hard for all of his accomplishments. He would apply his mental toughness to this new situation. He could be just as positive with one leg as he had been with two.

He didn't want any sympathy or pity. He wouldn't sulk or become depressed. He was so successful in thinking positively that when he had visitors he was the one to cheer them up. After a visit they usually left feeling higher than when they walked in.

"All the support I had from other people really helped me," Terry said. "Knowing that all those people cared. That and being really competitive. I decided I was going to beat it and get off my butt and show these people what I could do, that I could beat it and that I appreciated them coming to see me and that I was not all sad and gloom. So I decided that I would do my very best, that I would try to recuperate as fast as I could."

Some visitors felt apprehensive about seeing Terry. One of them was Terri Fleming, his basketball coach at PoCo, who wondered what he could say to a kid who was going to have his leg amputated the next day. Knowing Terry, he wanted to do something upbeat, so he found a recent issue of *Runner's World*, which included a story about an above-the-knee amputee, Dick Traum, who had run in the New York Marathon.

The coach didn't get much immediate reaction from Terry, but he hoped it would give the boy something to work over in his mind for a while.

That night a dream started germinating in Terry's brain. It wouldn't reach full flower for another three years, but the seed had been planted. That night an eighteen-year-old athlete who wasn't sure when he'd be able to walk again decided he wanted to run across Canada. He had already set himself another challenge. Sure, it was still a dream, but it drew him like a magnet.

"It was an impossible dream, a fantasy. That's what it was," Terry recalled. "I was lying in bed looking at this magazine, thinking if he can do it, I can do it, too. All it was was an impossibility, something that somebody else does. I didn't believe it. I didn't know if I'd even walk."

Terry found it difficult to explain why he fixed on such a magnificent dream, one on such a large scale. Why didn't he want to run in the New York Marathon or jog across British Columbia? Why Canada, the second largest country in the world?

"I don't know why I dreamed what I did. It's because I'm competitive. I'm a dreamer. I like challenges. I don't give up. That's why. When I decided to do it, I knew I was going to go all out. There was no in-between."

Judith arrived at work at 6 A.M. on March 9, the day of the operation, to let Terry know she was concerned about him and to give him some encouragement. She already looked on him as a younger brother. His surgery, scheduled for 8 A.M., would be the first of the day. Terry immediately showed Judith the magazine Terri Fleming had given him the night before. "Someday I'm going to do something like that," he said. His parents and brother Fred were at the hospital at 6 A.M., too.

Terry had been thoroughly examined to see if there were any other tumours. His lungs had been checked most carefully, since it is to that site that sarcoma cells most commonly drifted. The doctors, believing the tumour was contained, had decided to amputate Terry's leg above the knee instead of at the hip, which would have been a more crippling procedure.

Despite his doctors' caution, it's likely stray sarcoma cells, carried in his blood stream, were already resting in his lungs. As Louis Lichtenstein noted in his medical textbook *Bone Tumours*: "The discouraging outlook in dealing with osteogenic sarcoma does not appear to be attributable to any significant delay in its clinical recognition. What seems more probable, unfortunately, is that many patients with osteogenic sarcoma already have pulmonary seeding by the time they present themselves for treatment, even though their chest films appear negative."

The operation lasted about an hour. Terry's family doctor, Robert Heffelfinger, assisted Piper.

Terry didn't see his leg for a few days because it was wrapped in bandages.

When the bandages were removed he saw a stump, "swollen, awful, in sad shape." A tube to drain fluid had been inserted from his groin down to the sutures that enclosed the muscle and skin around the end of the bone.

Dr. Piper came several days later to check Terry over. Without a word of warning he ripped the tube out of Terry's leg. Those five seconds of pain were the most excruciating Terry had ever experienced, but all he said was "whew" and the doctor patted him on the back.

Terry received lots of encouragement from friends, family, and visitors, and from the cards — some from people he didn't even know – that were filling up his nightstand. His parents, perhaps, didn't accept the tragedy as easily as did Terry, but they did take it in stride; they had no other choice. There were lots of tears at home. Betty was still off work because of her foot operation. She would sniffle occasionally when she went back to the card shop, but tearful breakdowns were not her style. It was, however, difficult for her to talk about Terry, especially when a friend asked about him, and she made a great effort to be strong and not to show her hurt to others. And since Terry's attitude was so positive, it helped her accept his loss.

Terry wore his first artificial limb less than three weeks after the amputation. It was a temporary prosthesis because his stump was changing shape. He wouldn't get a permanent limb, which cost about $2,000, until the swelling stopped and the stump reached the size it was likely to remain. In the meantime Terry learned to walk on the primitive prosthesis, which included a plastic bucket shaped to resemble his mid-thigh and a flexible knee, but which lacked the springs his permanent leg would have. The stump was held in the socket by suction only and air was released manually through a valve in the bucket. The children on his ward – one of them, a boy who was in traction and couldn't walk for six weeks – cheered enthusiastically as Terry learned to walk.

"When I took the first step I felt as though I was stepping on air. It felt as if I was stepping on nothing, straight down. The first thing I said to myself was, 'How are you ever possibly going to walk?' Then I went to the washroom [where the children on the ward couldn't see] and sneaked another attempt, with crutches.

"I kept trying and trying until I could do more, I could feel more, I could step into it more, follow through more, until I could lift. Gradually I got to the point where I could use only one crutch and then only one cane. All the time we were waiting for the stump to shrink until I got my final leg."

Everyone kept looking for signs, for clues to Terry's adjustment. But there were no nightmares, no railings against society, no bitter denunciations of his parents, no rejections of old friends. Doug, who had been expecting some signs of depression, found none: "His attitude seemed to be it is gone, now get on with it."

Terri Fleming also noticed Terry's positive attitude, one that may well have assisted in his rapid healing.

"He took it so damn well," Fleming recalled. "I thought I'd see someone terrified, someone who had given up, but he just accepted it. He took it. I thought he was hiding it, that he was going to crack up, but he didn't."

Three weeks after he started using his artificial limb Terry was out with Rolly playing pitch-and-putt golf. The next challenge was an eighteen-hole golf course. Not long after that he would play twenty-seven holes in a day.

There were proud moments for his dad and Doug and for anyone who played golf with Terry in those early months. He was slow on the course, but he was getting very good at the game. It seemed to Doug that Terry could actually drive the ball farther than he could when he had had both legs. Although, according to Doug, anyone who saw Terry would swear he was aiming for the trees when he was teeing off. "He looked funny, he looked as if he was lined up wrong," Doug remembered. "All the weight was on his left leg and he held his body at an angle. You'd think he was going to hit the ball the wrong way."

The usual post-surgery follow-up (or adjuvant treatment) after the type of surgery Terry had is chemotherapy, which is intended to destroy any stray malignant cells before they multiply. Although doctors hadn't found any signs that the tumours had spread, without follow-up treatment, there was a 70-per-cent chance of recurrence. (The Mayo Clinic, which does not follow up with chemotherapy, reports a high, 50-percent-cure rate after surgery only. Following treatment of Edward Kennedy, Jr., chemotherapy was popularized in the mid-1970s and now is the usual course of treatment in most hospitals.)

A couple of weeks after his operation, Terry was admitted to the British Columbia Cancer Control Agency, commonly called the cancer clinic, in Vancouver for treatment he would receive every three weeks for fourteen months.

He was put on an experimental program to determine the most effective way of administering two proven cancer-killing drugs: adriamycin and Methotrexate. (Adriamycin is one of the anthracycline family of chemicals, while Methotrexate is a folic-acid antagonist, which blocks the action of folic acid, a vitamin-like substance needed for cell growth.) The two could be alternated or a treatment of adriamycin could be followed by a treatment of Methotrexate. Terry was given the alternating program.

The most immediately apparent reaction to the drug treatment was that Terry's hair fell out, a loss he said he felt more than the loss of his leg. He bought an inexpensive wig to hide his baldness, and no one except Darrell, who once caught him in the shower, ever saw him without it. The other side effect was nausea. Sometimes it lasted only overnight, but sometimes, with adriamycin, in particular, it lasted several days. Some patients say it's like having the flu. His appetite would be dulled for three or four more days, and then he would have three weeks at home to build up strength.

His doctors also had to watch that the drugs weren't harming his disease-fighting white blood cells and platelet-forming cells. They had to maintain a delicate balance to keep the dosage strong enough to kill the cancerous cells, but not the patient. The final, most frightening side effect, attributed to adriamycin, was increased risk of heart failure.

Terry went to the clinic the night before his Methotrexate treatment – adriamycin was usually administered as a shot – and would be fed fluids intravenously to get his kidneys working. Methotrexate, administered intravenously, was highly toxic, and would be excreted through his kidneys and his urine. He also chewed sodium bicarbonate pills to make his urine more alkaline and reduce the chances of Methotrexate crystals forming in his kidneys.

Methotrexate was given in a potent, potentially lethal dosage – one gram was enough to kill him and he was given between ten and fifteen grams in each treatment – but the drug was followed several hours later by an antidote, called leukovorin rescue, which was also fed into his bloodstream.

"The first time I took Methotrexate I wasn't sick. I just felt a little light-headed," Terry said. "After a while I got sicker and sicker. Even the sodium bicarbonate made me sick, and the leukovorin, when they started it two hours later, was getting me down."

Although Terry looked forward to his parents' visits, he didn't like them to come the first night of his treatment because he was too sick. After a while he would ask for an anti-nausea shot, which put him to sleep and took care of the first day. The second day, his parents would come and treat him to dinner at the Knight and Day, a restaurant on busy West Broadway.

The cancer clinic, where mortally ill patients were grim reminders of the statistics that two-thirds of cancer victims died of the disease, was a different world from the pediatric ward at the Royal Columbian. Terry saw himself as the healthiest person in the clinic, but rather than crushing his spirit, the sight of others' suffering made him stronger. He took the treatment in a four-patient room divided only by curtains. While he drew the curtains for privacy when he was vomiting after chemotherapy treatment, some of the other patients didn't. Although the atmosphere was intended to be supportive, on the theory that somehow the patient felt better knowing the guy in the next bed had the same problems that he did, Terry detested the openness. "You could hear their stories, you could hear what was happening to them, what their situation was, what their reactions with their families were and I didn't like that. There was no privacy. When I got sick, I wanted to be sick by myself and I couldn't.

"You could hear doctors telling these guys, 'You've got a 15-per-cent chance to live,' and this type of thing. I really didn't like that part of the hospital for that reason. I spent as much time out of the room as I could.

"It was just a really dull, dull place, but I have nothing but respect for the doctors and nurses. They have a lot of courage, and there aren't a lot of miracles there."

Judith Ray had warned Terry about the clinic and the side effects of the treatment, but nothing could prepare him for what he called the "grossities" of cancer – the swelling of a tumour on a young man's neck, the emaciation. He'd talk to Judith about it when he visited her back at the Royal Columbian. "It shook him up," she said. "There were people in the same ward as him who had the same problem as he did, and it was obvious some of them were dying. That reinforced the reality of what he was up against. Even that didn't put him down, though. It gave him motivation to really fight, because he saw people there were really suffering. I suppose in a way it's unusual – he's a real natural fighter and worked hard for everything he's gotten or done – but there are a lot of people like that who, if you encourage them when they're down, are able to maintain that thrust forward."

During the interim weeks at home, Terry liked to keep life as normal as possible, as it had been. Betty, however, would bustle around the house trying to move things out of his way and cater to him as she never had before, spoiling him just a little. She'd bring him food and drinks on a tray, even when he was capable of getting them himself. He soon convinced her that he didn't need or want special treatment. He was so successful in his attitude that Darrell can hardly remember his being sick. He certainly never considered the possibility that Terry might not live.

Neither did his parents, even though they were not ignorant of the reality of his condition. Whenever he went to a doctor's appointment, Betty and Rolly joined him. When he went to the cancer clinic, they went, too, asking questions all the time.

Although Terry may have seemed much the same to his younger brother, he experienced a profound change. He told a story about a twenty-two-year-old from the Okanagan who, for a while, shared his room at the clinic. He had Hodgkin's disease, a malignancy in the lymph glands, and he was riddled with tumours. "They gave him a chemotherapy treatment over the night, and the drug they gave him cleared his chest completely. It was just fantastic. He was so happy; they were letting him go home for a week. Then I saw the same guy about six months later . . . and he was just nothing. I was lying in my bed one night and I could hear a guy screaming in pain at different times. I got up to go to the washroom, and they were bringing him back in a wheelchair. He had tubes hooked up everywhere. I thought it was him and then I knew it was when I saw his name on an X-ray form. He was so thin and weak and fragile. He couldn't recognize me. He was probably drugged up. He was in a chair breathing, 'Help me, help me,' and that just hurt me. I saw that end of it a lot, but I hadn't seen the beginning. I hadn't seen the person healthy.

"There were a few other cases, too, people I'd seen progress. It was awful, sometimes, the stories. We talked about it. We had to talk, and it was hard, it was so hard – the pain in the faces and the situations people were in, with their families there and the whole thing.

"It's awful but that's happening right now, all over the world in every city, in every town, one out of every fourth person. That experience was really a motivator."

On the last day of his treatment, the nurses brought Terry a little cake and celebrated his release. Until that time, Terry's universe had been small. He had his basketball, his university work, a couple of buddies, and a caring family. He liked to watch the B.C. Lions and the Vancouver Canucks. He liked to go to the movies. He liked Chinese food. He believed that most things in life – a good job, marriage, children – were within his grasp.

Although he said, "All I thought of was myself," he was probably no more or less self-centred than any other teenager. He hadn't spent much time reflecting on the human condition. He had no reason for such thoughts. He was a nice, ordinary sort of kid, who was honest, followed a strict moral code of his own choosing, worked hard, but was not unusually compassionate or caring. "I've always had a bad temper and I think I've hurt people at times because of it. When I was younger, especially before I had my cancer, maybe I'd take advantage of people. Even though I was motivated and I tried hard and did my best, made the SFU team and did well in school, I only did it because I wanted to achieve it myself. I would do anything, even hurt other people if I had to, to achieve that. But the clinic – that's what changed me."

Other cancer patients would show the same strength as Terry because their ordeal demanded strength, but he took his experiences one step farther. He'd seen despair and not succumbed to it; he'd seen disease kick the fighting spirit out of young men, yet he felt tougher, mentally, than he had before cancer; and he'd seen death, yet was still alive. Believing he had beat the 50- to 70-per-cent chances of survival, Terry experienced a form of rebirth. So he didn't skip out of the clinic after the celebratory cake with a mere round of thank-yous to the doctors and nurses. Since he was part of the lucky one-third of patients who survived cancer, Terry felt a sense of responsibility. He firmly believed in the value of traditional cancer research. After all, it had helped him beat the disease. Since he was alive and reasonably healthy, he believed he had a debt to repay, not just for himself, but for all the others who later filled his sick bed. Terry became more than compassionate, he became committed and decided that others would be able to find courage in his example.

"Nobody," he said, "is ever going to call me a quitter."

# Chapter Four

Rick Hansen was uneasy about making the call. He'd heard via the grapevine about the SFU basketball player who had lost a leg, and he wondered if Terry would be interested in playing wheelchair basketball for the Vancouver Cablecars. That summer in 1977, Rick, a superb athlete himself although he was a paraplegic and needed crutches to walk, worked for the Canadian Wheelchair Sports Association. Part of his job was to recruit players; sometimes it wasn't easy, especially since he could never tell how recently disabled person would react to the idea of wheelchair sport.

Rick saw the sport as a tough discipline, as challenging as any sport for able-bodied players. A physical-education student at the University of British Columbia, Rick had developed his chest and his arm and shoulder muscles to such an extent that they seemed to swell out of his T-shirts. Rick, like Terry, was a hard worker. Part of his training was to push himself twenty miles a day in his wheelchair.

When Rick picked up the phone and spoke to Terry, a connection was made. Terry listened as Rick explained that he had been an athlete before his accident, and that now, despite the loss of use of his legs, he was still an athlete. He suggested Terry might want a little exercise and offered to bring a wheelchair for him to the next practice.

Terry was interested. He sensed in Rick the one quality to which he would always respond: Rick, too, pushed himself to the limit.

When Terry turned up at the Renfrew Community Centre for the next practice, he came with Rolly, Betty, and Judith. His family was behind him in more than spirit. Peter Colistro, a polio victim whose right leg was in a brace and who would later become Terry's close friend, was shocked at the appearance of the newest team member. To Peter, Terry was so white and thin he looked like a scarecrow. He seemed like a fourteen- or fifteen-year-old instead of a nineteen-year-old; his hair was long, stringy, and flat, just the sort you'd see sticking out of a strawman's hat. No one, of course, knew that Terry was undergoing chemotherapy every three weeks and that he was wearing a wig.

Terry started practising lay-ups immediately, although he was a little shaky in the wheelchair. He was amazed, in fact, that the men could actually do the basketball drills from wheelchairs and that they could make the basket. On his first few tries, Terry couldn't come close to the rim, but by the end of the practice, he made two lay-ups in a row. The other players could tell immediately that Terry had good skills. He just had to learn to gear his basketball reflexes, which were directed to his legs, up to his arms. He was always trying to jump to his feet to get the ball. Rick explained that Terry had to redevelop his neuro-muscular pathways; instead of moving with his feet, as his instinct told him, he had to move with his hands.

According to the modified rules for wheelchair basketball, he was allowed five seconds in the key instead of the usual three seconds, and he had to dribble the ball if he took more than two pushes on his wheelchair. He had to strap himself into the chair to keep from jumping for the ball. Just as though he were back in Bob McGill's grade eight basketball practice, Terry had to learn all over again. Again, he was the thirteenth man on a thirteen-man team.

But not for long. His soft palms toughened up. They blistered, and the blisters broke, bled and then calloused over.

Mike McNeill from Simon Fraser University watched him as he struggled to improve himself in a wheelchair. Once McNeill caught Terry as he came into the gym and he stopped dead. "Jesus, Terry, look at your hands," he said. Terry looked down and saw the scrapes. Cuts ran across his palms, and his fingertips, McNeill recalled, "were all chewed up." McNeill's concern baffled Terry. He was happy and it simply was not in his nature to complain. He was doing what he wanted.

Within two months of joining the Cablecars, Terry was picked to go to the national wheelchair basketball games held in Edmonton in August. In those months he had climbed from thirteenth to sixth place on the team.

While he was in Edmonton, it was arranged for Terry to take a chemotherapy treatment at the University of Alberta hospital. As a result, Peter Colistro, who accompanied Terry, learned about Terry's condition. One of the attending doctors quietly told Peter.

"Is he that bad, Doc?" Peter asked. He was bluntly told how sick Terry was and that Terry shouldn't have even travelled with the team to Edmonton. For the first time Peter came to terms with the notion that Terry might not have long to live. Everything fell into place: Terry's emanciated appearance, how he sometimes fell asleep on the sidelines during a game, the doctor's concern.

Despite all that, the Cablecars won the nationals – they've claimed the title ten times in the past twelve years – and Terry helped. In fact, he eventually played on three championship winning teams.

Terry's team mates kept their worry about him to themselves. Terry, for his part, did not want sympathy and did not want to be treated differently. However, there was a slight problem with the wig. Rick Hansen recalled this story: "I used to pat Terry on the head if he'd make a good play, and I thought it was strange that every time I patted him, he'd reach up and touch his hair. We went down to Portland for a tournament, and were brutally beaten by Los Angeles in a preseason game. While we were showering I noticed that even though Terry was standing right under the water, his hair wasn't getting wet. Terry noticed me looking and said, 'I'm going to have to tell you something. You know when you pat me on the head, I don't want you to tell anyone, but I'm wearing a wig and I'm afraid you're going to knock it off!'

"From then on, I patted him on the shoulder. But about a month or so later, back home during a team practice, Terry was in the middle of a scramble for the ball and there were five guys around him. He had the ball and was moving around so no one could check him. One of the big guys, Gene Reimer, a weight-lifter, took a swipe at the ball and then all I saw was this wig come sailing out of the scrimmage. First came the wig, then came Terry, diving after it and plastering it on his head as fast as he could. His face was beet red."

It was the most colour they'd seen in him since he joined the team. When the moment of awkward silence broke into jockish laughter, Terry's was the loudest.

When the fuzz started appearing on his head, he turned to wearing baseball caps, and had trouble with one referee who objected to a baseball cap on a basketball player. The referee so upset Terry he didn't play very well, Peter remembered.

Soon Terry was a motivator for the other wheelchair basketball players. His competitive spirit spurred the same instincts in Rick, Peter, and their team mates. He pestered them, he pushed them, he irritated them. He called them slackers, and his intensity infected everyone. Because he was a student at SFU he arranged gym time so the wheelchair players could practise more. He simply couldn't understand that some of the men on the team were there just for fun, and he was disappointed if they didn't share his competitve zeal.

His body changed, too. His hair was back, this time in luxuriant curls. His torso thickened and became muscular. He had changed, Rick recalled, "from a skinny little runt to a strapping fellow with lots of beef and muscle." He also had his own wheelchair, a gift from Rolly's workmates in the Canadian National Railway yard.

By the 1979-80 season, the Cablecars were rated sixth in the North American Wheelchair basketball association. Both Terry and Peter were chosen as guards for the all-star team. It was an honour, but Terry, as usual, felt he could have played better.

Later, at the Wheelchair Olympics, held in Arnhem, Holland, in 1980, Peter was chosen for the Olympic all-star team, meaning he was one of the five best wheelchair players in the world. He graciously gave credit to Terry, among others, for helping him reach that standard of excellence. In the same competition Rick set a world record in the 800-metre spring in his wheelchair and won a gold medal.

Wheelchair basketball took up three nights of the week. Terry, however, was used to a more challenging regime. Since one wasn't set out in wheelchair basketball, he set one for himself. By mid-1978 he was pushing himself hard to strengthen his arms and hands. He'd go anywhere in his wheelchair that provided a challenge. Some days found him hurtling along the sea-wall around Vancouver's dense and lovely Stanley Park. He set out past the marina near the lavish Bayshore Hotel and circled round until he could see Burrard Inlet, which stretched long and far down to Port Moody. He pushed hard past the statue of the little mermaid, and then continued under the great arch of the Lions Gate Bridge. To his left loomed centuries' old stands of fir and cedar, and to his right were the great freighters, the sturdy trawlers, and tugs chugging towards the Vancouver docks. It was perhaps one of the loveliest walks in Canada, a favourite of joggers, Sunday afternoon hikers, and lovers any season of the year. To Terry, those joggers and strollers were markers and challenges; his goal always was to get by them as quickly as possible.

He set more difficult goals for himself. One more isolated and many times more difficult than the sea-wall was the steep Westwood Mountain, which lay not far from his home and led to a go-cart and automobile race track. The top of the hill had been logged, and the rough logging trucks cut up the road and made driving difficult and slow.

Sometimes his father would drive Terry to the foot of the hill, drop him off and go to the top to wait for him. Sometimes Terry tackled the hill two or three times in one session. His best time was fifteen minutes.

Once in a while, Doug, who was training for cross-country running, would race with him to the top. They wouldn't so much race against each other, Terry in a wheelchair and Doug on his two legs, as challenge each other. "I just wanted to compete against someone," Terry said. "I didn't want to compete just against the hill. Knowing that Doug – or anyone, even a dog – was coming up behind me was just what I needed to go my hardest. I used him to push me harder."

Nonetheless, it must have been a startling scene: Terry breathing hard and heavy after a head start, his arms doing the work of Doug's legs, and Doug setting out just a few minutes later, doing his damnedest to conquer that mile and possibly Terry.

On clear days from the top, Terry could see the familiar snow-capped cone of Mount Baker in Washington state towering on the horizon. Sometimes the whole valley, a blanket of evergreen, stretched out before him; sometimes the lowlands would be obscured by fog. Mostly, though, it would simply rain, and Terry, drenched and determined, just kept on wheeling.

His third challenge was Burnaby Mountain. A road winds for close to three miles up it to Simon Fraser University. It's called

Gaglardi Way, after the Social Credit minister of transport in W.A.C. Bennett's cabinet known as Flying Phil Gaglardi, and it cuts a four-lane swath through the spindly birch that in mild winters sometimes stays green until December. It's not as steep as Westwood but it's three times as long, and the abandoned Volkswagens that litter its curb lane are evidence of its difficulty.

Students driving up to use the library or gym on weekends were sometimes struck by a peculiar movement on the side of the road. One of them described it as a moving box, until he got close enough to recognize Terry in his wheelchair. Terry's best time was usually about thirty minutes, which he could check against the clock tower when he reached the top of the hill. Sometimes he'd ask Doug, Rick, or Peter to drive him back to his car at the bottom of the hill because he could rub his hands raw trying to hold back the wheelchair on a downward slope. "Sometimes I was stupid and I'd do it on my own," said Terry. "Sometimes I'd come down in the pouring rain and couldn't get a grip on the wheels. They just slipped through my hands. Once I hitchhiked down. I just sat in the wheelchair and stuck out my thumb. The first guy who passed me stopped."

Terry didn't understand why this part of his story stuck so firmly in everyone's mind, especially those of reporters. Being so pragmatic, he didn't see the romance, the startling excess of his challenge. He saw that wearying climb simply as another part of his training. To him, it was no more of an achievement than the long, dull hours he spent circling the SFU gym in his wheelchair. All that he remembered was that he was training alone, without a coach, without one of his motivators, going around and around and around the empty gym with the single-minded, perhaps obsessive dedication that had become his trademark.

Next Terry tried running. Since he was active in wheelchair sports, he raced in the association's annual summer games. He remembered his first try at competitive running: "I was going to run a hundred metres, and a guy named Dan, who's a double amputee and uses crutches, was going to crutch a hundred metres. But since there were two of us they threw us in the same heat. Even though we were in different competitions, we were put in the same heat.

"I ran as fast as I could go – and I can run fast, can get going pretty good when I just sprint, you know – and my knee broke

43

right in half, right in half, and I went flying after only about ten metres. I went flying in the air and I landed on the ground. Danny went by me, crutching away. It took him about a minute and a half to finish 100 metres and he said, 'At least I beat Terry.' That was funny."

While Terry was quite capable of looking after his body and its training, there wasn't anyone helping him look after his soul, and it needed a little work as well. Or it did until Rika Noda, a Japanese-Canadian and stained-glass artist, caught his eye. Rika had a little studio built in the back of her bedroom in the basement of her parents' split-level home overlooking the Fraser River. There she practised her craft and exercised her whimsy – among her stained-glass works was a miniature rendering of the Hickory-Dickory-Dock nursery rhyme, complete with mice, and red hearts dangling from the chimes of the grandfather clock. She still kept stuffed toys, including a Snoopy, tossed on her bed, not far from the bookshelf filled with Bibles, books on the spiritual life, and books on sports from her course on recreational leadership at Langara college. Rika was petite and vivacious and, like Terry, seemed younger than her twenty years. Her liveliness complemented his shyness.

Rika heard about Terry some time before she met him. She was an assistant coach for the Canadian Wheelchair Volleyball Association, and since some of the volleyball players also played basketball, they told her about the SFU basketball player who was now a whiz on the wheelchair team. One evening the volleyball players took Rika to the Renfrew Community Centre to watch a basketball game. She spotted Terry immediately. He was the one, in her eyes, who seemed to be playing harder and better than the others. She didn't fail to notice, either, that he was very handsome, especially with his recently arrived crop of brown curls.

He noticed her, too, and within a few weeks started playing wheelchair volleyball, though his interest in volleyball waned while interest in Rika flourished. He would drive her home from practice, and one night he asked her out, very formally – for that is usually a shy person's manner – to dinner at the Sears Harbour House.

Rika, a girl who felt most comfortable in jeans or corduroy overalls and sneakers, and who was happiest doing her work sitting cross-legged on the floor, was surprised at the solemnity of the invitation, but quickly accepted. She had found a dress to wear for the night, and as they walked to the elevator of the revolving restaurant, Terry took her hand. The city of Vancouver moved at their feet. They continued to hold hands and spoke not of their incipient romance, but of a topic close to Rika's heart – God's love.

Rika was a Christian. Terry had snickered long and loudly at the "television Christians" whose ministries are conducted, as he said, with "perfect hair-dos, perfect clothes, and perfect plastic smiles." He didn't like the praise-the-Lord approach to divinity, but he was interested in Rika's style of Christianity. She believed in God, that Christ had died for all mankind, and that the Bible held the key to eternal life. She was warm, exuberant, and she didn't sledgehammer him with fundamentalism. Just as Terry had been sent to Sunday School as a child, Rika had been sent to a Buddhist temple. Later, she attended Christian services. She said she became a Christian when she was nine and had a child's faith but lacked adult understanding. That came later, when she experienced a "sanctification," as she called it, and developed a "personal relationship with God." As she grew closer to Terry, she hoped that he would experience the same illumination, not only for his own sake but also because she believed that as a Christian, she should not go out with boys who had not embraced Christ as she had. But she had found that Terry, with his competitive instincts and shy manners, was simply irresistible. She was hooked.

Terry was hooked on what she had to say. She started taking him to the Ruth Morton Baptist Church, which she attended. In fact, Sundays were the busiest days of her week. Rika urged Terry to read the Bible and he did.

She was one of the few people to whom he could talk about cancer. Cancer and his experiences at the clinic had introduced a new, thoughtful side to Terry. Though his philosophy was still immature in that it lacked depth, he didn't lack in striving. Terry was a seeker. "I guess I was searching for something, for an answer," he recalled. "I had just finished treatment and had a lot of questions: why did I get cancer and not someone else? I was starting to think about life. I was getting older, too, thinking about different attitudes towards life. I didn't know how I could apply those attitudes in my life. I was looking for an answer to the question why?

Although Rika was cheering Terry on his spiritual path, he still felt torn, divided between his old loyalties and his new ones. None of his friends was an active believer. His parents were not church-goers; they had felt a certain bitterness ever since the death of Betty's sister Norma.

"I worried about what my family thought. Even if I wanted to change my life, none of my friends was interested in it, and I couldn't forget about them all. I couldn't block them out. I wanted them. Yet I almost felt I had to do that – block them out – to devote myself to it. It's always difficult to be different from the norm. To me, just starting to read the Bible was different from what anyone else in my family was doing."

Throughout these months, Terry harboured his dream of run-ning across Canada, but, as he said, it wasn't the right time. He was strong, but he had run very little and had yet to develop his stamina. The most rigorous training of his life lay before him.

Three-year-old Terry Fox posed for a photograph with his brother Fred (right) and Santa Claus.

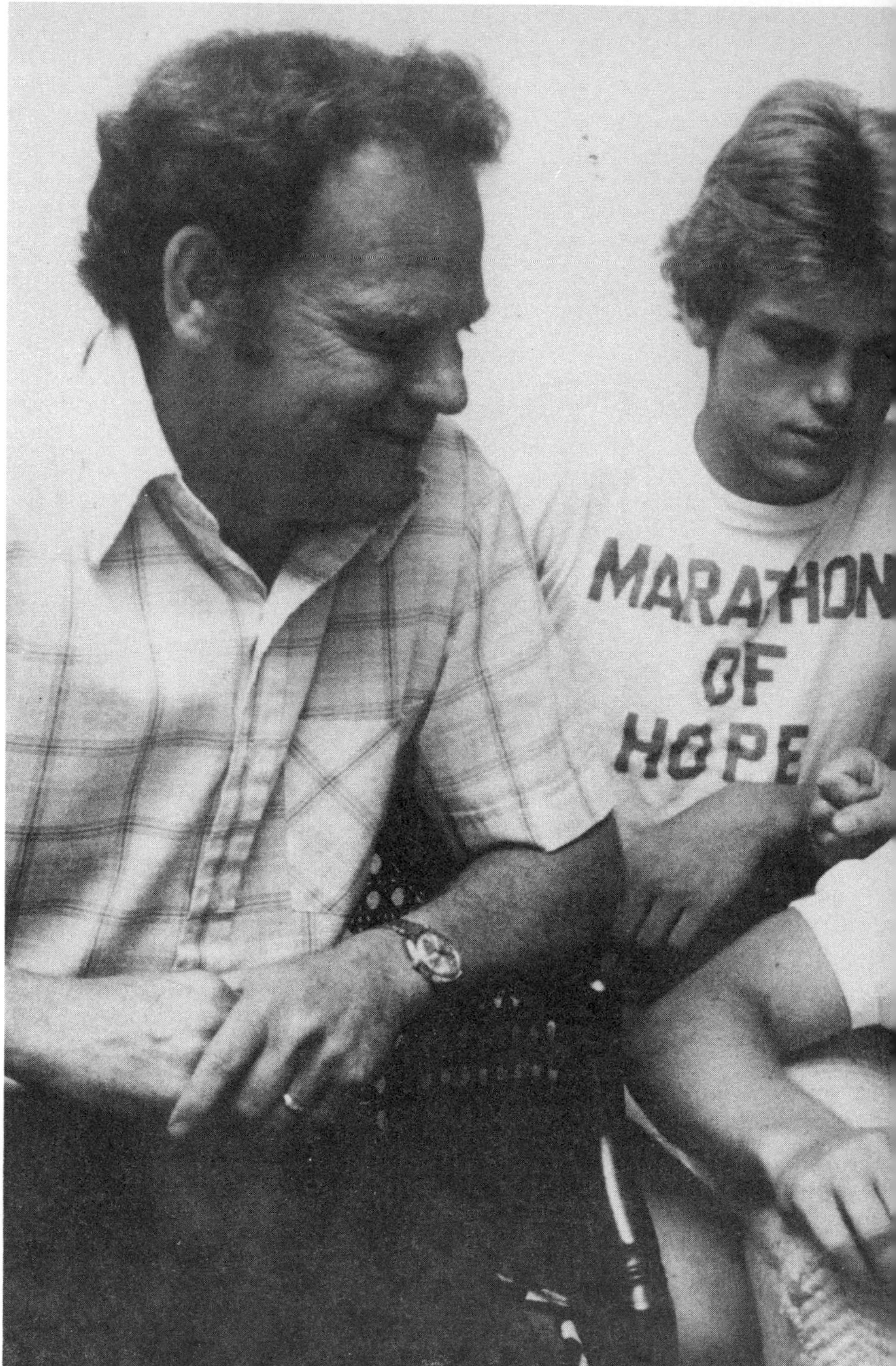
MARATHON
OF
HOPE

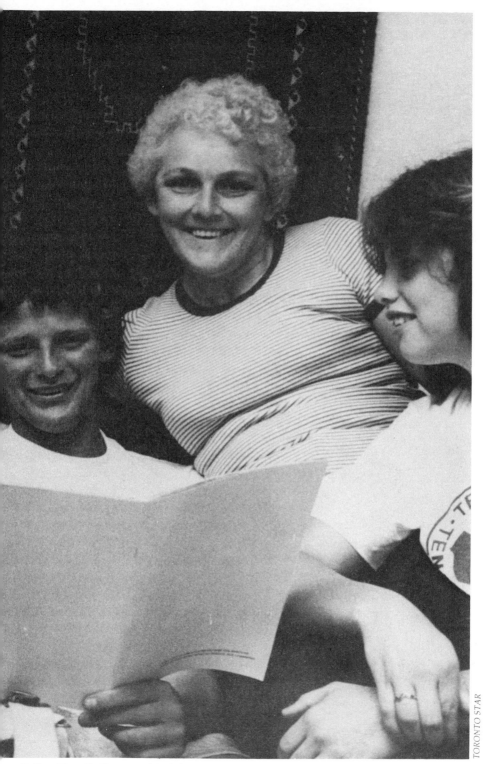

Rolly, Darrell, Betty and Judith Fox share a quiet moment in Toronto with Terry.

Terry Fox, holding the ball on the right, had an early and lasting interest in athletic achievement. The Ravens, the Port Coquitlam Senior Secondary's basketball team, are shown here in their annual photograph.

Some of Terry's proudest moments during his Marathon of Hope were his participation in sports events, such as this opening pitch at a Blue Jay's game in Toronto.

Although Terry's achievement was enormous in its scope – both in terms of miles run and dollars raised – it was accomplished one step and one mile at a time.

TORONTO STAR

The support and encouragement of people along the way meant a lot to Terry.
In Pickering, Ontario, he was applauded by John and Edna Neale.

By the time Terry crossed the border from Quebec into Ontario, his Marathon of Hope had captured the interest and imagination of many.

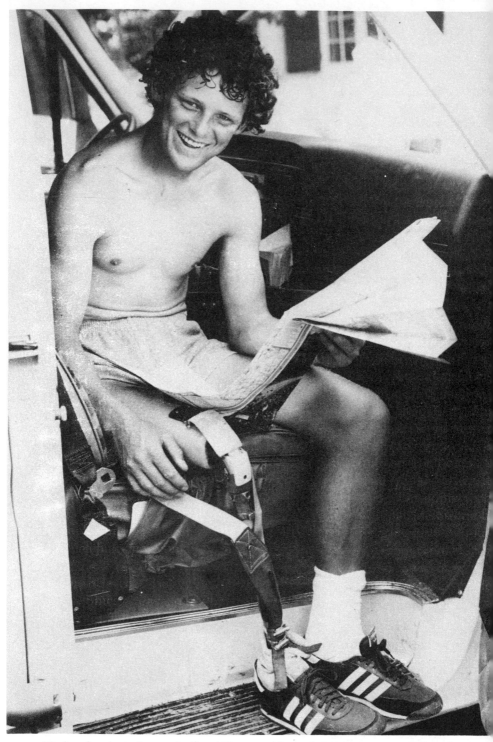

His breaks along the road offered Terry much-needed time to rest and plan the route ahead.

# Chapter Five

In January 1979, Terry started a diary. It was a modest, pocket-sized volume, made in Korea, and covered in vinyl. He wrote his name, address, SFU student number, and phone number in the front cover. Terry didn't reflect about life or himself in its pages. He always insisted that he was no writer, although there were times when he could be disarmingly articulate. His first entries served more as a daily reminder and as a record of his school assignments:

> *January 4. Scholarship. Books. Basketball. Phone auto places.*
> *January 14. Continue Kin. 467 reading. Basketball. Think*
>     *about 320 essay if can't figure out, see T.A. on Tuesday.*
> *January 27. Kin. 467 reread chapter, underline reread notes,*
>     *memorize, continue lab.*
> *February 10. Wheel up mountain. Bring Rika get her to type*
>     *essay.*

Gradually, Terry began to record his running:

> *February 5. ½ mile, weights.*

Terry ran his first half mile around the cinder track at Hastings Junior High School, the school Judith attended. It was about six blocks from his home. Four laps around the track, which was lined on three sides with great fir stands, equaled one mile. "It was hard, it was hard. The first few half miles especially. I remember on my third time or so, I was just dead, completely dead. Sweating, wiped out. I would usually run at night then."

Seven days later Terry ran his first mile. "The first day I ran a mile was as great as the first day I ran thirty miles because to me it was phenomenal. Here I was, getting healthy and active and getting strong and running hard. In shorter distances you naturally run faster. In fact, one day, I remember running past two-legged people who were jogging. That helped me and made me feel so great. You know, I enjoyed it. I really was glad I was able to do that.

"I was weight-lifting as well, at the time, and I was building my strength up. My body was getting bigger, my leg was getting bigger. I was getting healthier and in better condition and feeling more positive all the time. Each time I ran a further distance, was able to run a further half mile, it was great because I was improving all the time and I was able to keep going."

Terry worked with his prosthetist Ben Speicher on developing a better running-leg. Speicher devised a pogo stick with a motorcycle's shock absorber to give Terry more oomph with each step, but he didn't like it. So they reverted to a more traditional leg reinforced and modified to take the punishment of long-distance running. The metal valve in the bucket was replaced with one of stainless steel so it wouldn't rust from perspiration. Speicher added a belt that fitted around Terry's waist and attached to an elastic strap at the knee to bring the leg forward more quickly after each stride.

In addition to the ordinary fatigue felt by two-legged runners, Terry had special problems. His good leg suffered from the extra pounding he gave it. He developed blisters on his foot and cysts on his stump.

"I had some bad blisters, man. Oh boy, it was just like running on coals. I really had some sores on my leg where the artificial leg was. They just rubbed raw and there's no protection at all. Sometimes the sores would bleed right through my valve in the bucket and the blood would run all down my knee and my leg and I had it all over me."

Sometimes merely adjusting his leg to a more comfortable position would bring some slight relief, but he was always searching for just the right technique, the right motion that would make the running easier and the pain less intense.

"One of the harder times was when I went from running on a cinder track to cement, because running on cement was so hard on my body, especially my foot. I developed bone bruises. My toes and heel were totally blistered, like raw, and I lost three toenails, all because of running on cement. I had shin splints for two months, a sharp pain in my lower leg. I did it all gradually. If I hadn't I would have probably broken my leg. I was fortunate. Here was where stubbornness came through. I knew the toenails would grow back in and would be okay. The blisters, I knew, were eventually going to turn to callouses, but I was afraid of the bone bruise because I could have gotten stress fractures. But I kept going and it went away.

"Usually the pain came in different stages. A lot of times the very beginning is the hard part. You have to take the first fifteen or twenty minutes to get warmed up. Then you get over a pain threshold. That's what I did a lot. You'd still have the pain and blisters, and sometimes it would get a little worse and then not so bad again, but it never was unbearable. There were times when it really hurt, but I kept going. I can't remember ever being in so much pain for such a long time that I had to stop. I never did."

Through these months, only Doug knew that Terry was dreaming of running across Canada. (Doug's personal goal was the Prince George Marathon, held on Labour Day weekend. The runner with the best time earned a ticket to the Boston Marathon.) Terry had phoned Doug in the spring and asked for general advice about running and sometimes they would run together. Doug recalled, "He wanted my advice, but wouldn't listen to it. I thought he ate too much meat and salad: you can't get calories from that. He was stubborn and we'd fight and argue, but after a while he might bend a bit. His dream of running across Canada didn't seem odd to me. He just told me what he wanted to do, and then we started talking about training. I guess I never looked at him as having an artificial leg. Having one leg may have made it a little more difficult, but when Terry said he was going to do something he did it. After all, he made the basketball team. He wasn't one to make phony promises. If anyone could run across Canada, he could. But I didn't think training would be as difficult as it was. Even I didn't know what it was like to run twenty miles a day. At my best, when I was training for Prince George, I ran up to sixty miles a week."

Later Terry told Rika his dream of running across Canada. Both his friends seemed to have accepted Terry's goal almost unthinkingly. Rika, used to Terry's enthusiastic determination, believed Terry could do it. "He had to do something so monumental to prove to himself more than anything else that he could do it. Of course, he wanted to raise money for cancer, but I think more than anything it was a really big personal battle."

Rika was finding her relationship with Terry enormously taxing. She was in love with him, but realized he didn't feel the same way. He told her he didn't have the time to spend with a girlfriend because he wanted to concentrate totally on his running. He still enjoyed her companionship and hoped they could be friends. Rika, however, felt he sometimes took advantage of her good nature, especially when he picked her up, took her to his house, and set her to work typing his English essays while he watched television. Terry was shocked and hurt by the notion that Rika felt used. "I believed she wanted to help me because she was my friend," he explained simply.

Rika, like Betty Fox, found it difficult to get angry with Terry. She adored his honesty and spontaneous, though sometimes explosive, emotions. Beneath his grumpiness she saw a certain purity and she didn't want to lose him. She knew the relationship was unfair to her, but she accepted his terms because she was still so fond of him.

By June, Terry realized his priorities had shifted so much that, even with Rika's help, he was falling behind in his classwork. For an overachiever, that was difficult to bear. He gave himself a pep talk in his diary:

> Get to work at 401 lab. Let's do it, Terry, it is important. As important as running.

And as one sometimes given to excess, he followed that command with a row of fat, wobbly exclamation points.

By August 11 he was running ten miles a day and had lost two toenails. He could race up Westwood Mountain two times in a row, and some days he would alternate that with a seven-mile evening run around Stanley Park.

On August 30, Terry left with Doug, Darrell, Rika, and Rick Hansen for Prince George. He had decided to run half the seventeen-mile marathon because so far he hadn't run more than eleven miles a day. But Doug was picking away at him.

Doug's soft voice got under his skin. He persisted and gnawed at Terry. He kept asking Terry why he only wanted to go eight and a half miles: he could run that at home any day he wanted. Why travel 500 miles to do something that he could do practically in his own backyard? Why not make it an event? Why not try for seventeen miles? Terry went for it again.

Doug came eighth in the race, which was one of his best. Darrell placed second in the junior race. Terry came last, with a time of three hours, nine minutes, running close to eleven-minute miles. What made him chuckle with pride was that the last two-legged runner finished only ten minutes ahead of him. Some of the organizers worried about Terry's running so far and discussed forcing him to stop running. They didn't actually approach him, and Terry insisted that even if they had, nothing could have held him back. Nothing.

No one could have deprived him of that moment when he crossed the finish line and heard a crowd of maybe a hundred people standing to cheer and honour him. Terry's confidence was unshakeable after that. He never doubted his abilities, but when he heard that roar of commendation, when he saw fellow athletes weeping with admiration, he learned that each of his steps carried an emotional punch. That night at the awards banquet, the winner acknowledged that what affected him most was the sight of the tough little amputee runner.

When they all arrived home from Prince George, Betty walked out to the driveway to welcome them. Terry was still jubilant from the warm reception he'd received from the other runners. That meeting characterized the closeness between mother and son. Even later, when telling the anecdote to others, Betty's eyes would fill with tears and the words would catch in her throat. She remembered Terry's excitement and how he couldn't tell her quickly enough all that had happened.

Then he said to her, "I wish you'd been there, Mom. It was the biggest day of my life!"

Betty wondered, for a long time after, why they hadn't gone to watch him.

A few days later, back home, Terry and Doug were driving along the Barnet Highway into Vancouver to go to the movies. Terry said that he thought he was ready to try the cross-Canada run. Doug, pragmatic, non-plussed, almost immovable, said "When?" That's all. Originally they had thought it would take two years of training, but Terry was bursting with confidence and strength, and two years seemed an awfully long time. Then Doug

suggested, simply, "Why not try for next spring?" It seemed star-
tlingly clear and they agreed. Terry took three days' rest and then
he started running. This time he was training to run across
Canada.

Those were difficult days for Terry and his family. First he had
to break the news to Betty. She and Rolly still didn't know about
his dream. He waited two weeks before telling his mother. They
were sitting alone in their living room. Betty was on the stuffed
colonial-style couch. Terry was in front of the picture window, sitting in the massive matching chair made for long hours of comfort
in front of the colour television. It was dark, and he was about to
start his second run of the day. He'd done ten miles in the morning
and had another four and a half to go.

The conversation, which was restrained (the Foxes are not prone
to windy explanations; they say their piece and then wait for the
world to fall apart), went something like this:

"Mom, I'm going to run across Canada."

"You are not."

"Yes, I am."

"Terry, you are not!"

Terry shouted that he was going to do it anyway and she'd better get behind him.

Betty remembered the next part. "I probably told him it was a
dumb, crazy idea. Why not run across B.C.? Run marathons. He
went out madder than a hatter, slamming the door behind him."

Betty was left in tears again. She was also left with the responsibility of telling Rolly. She waited about a week and, finding a
quiet moment, went down to the family room.

"Sit there and listen," she said to Rolly. "Don't yell." Then she
told him about Terry's plans.

Rolly, who had sensed that something important was being kept
from him, merely said, "When?" Knowing Terry, what else could
he say?

Betty was by now convinced that she was the only Fox with any
common sense. She wondered if Terry really knew how much
work and money it would take to run across Canada. Apparently
he did. He had sounded out his idea on Colin Johnstone, chaplain
at the cancer clinic, and on the same day had walked into the office
of Blair MacKenzie, executive director of the British Columbia and
Yukon Division of the Canadian Cancer Society, and told him he

wanted to raise money for cancer research. Blair was sceptical. Every year, a handful of men and women who want to do good approach the society for sponsorship, but Blair usually found there were strings attached. To test their sincerity, he told them the society would give them no financial support, but that if they found sponsors then he might talk business. Usually Blair never heard from them again.

As for Terry, Blair believed his dream of raising one million dollars was impossible.

To Terry, however, the task Blair set him was a simple one. Once he knew what was expected, he sat down with Rika and together they composed a letter – using Terry's ideas and Rika's grammar – which they sent to Imperial Oil, the Ford Motor Company, Adidas, and several other companies, requesting gas, a vehicle, running shoes, and money, respectively. His letter read:

The night before my amputation, my former basketball coach brought me a magazine with an article on an amputee who ran in the New York Marathon. It was then when I decided to meet this new challenge head on and not only overcome my disability, but conquer it in such a way that I could never look back and say it disabled me. But I soon realized that would only be half of my quest, for as I went through the sixteen months of the physically and emotionally draining ordeal of chemotherapy, I was rudely awakened by the feelings that surrounded and coursed throughout the cancer clinic. There were the faces with the brave smiles, and the ones who had given up smiling. There were the feelings of hopeful denial, and the feelings of despair. My quest would not be a selfish one. I could not leave knowing these faces and feelings would still exist, even though I would be set free from mine. Somewhere the hurting must stop . . . and I was determined to take myself to the limit for this cause. . . .

By April next year I will be ready to achieve something that for me was once only a distant dream reserved for the world of miracles; to run across Canada to raise money for the fight against cancer. . . . I'm not saying that this will initiate any kind of definitive answer or cure to cancer, but I believe in miracles. I have to.

During those 101 days, Terry's stubbornness flamed into proportions never before imagined. He'd pick Betty up at work, and as she sat beside him in the car she'd see blood oozing out of his valve and down his knee. His socks would be drenched in blood. She bit her lip to keep from crying or saying anything that might upset him. She knew from experience that the wrong word would light up Terry's temper like a Roman candle. So she kept her own counsel.

Sometimes she felt Terry was downright nasty in his obsession to run, but she understood that he often got overheated and acted without thinking. Besides, she sometimes thought, that temperament ran in the family. He was never malicious, or purposely unkind, it was just that he wanted life to go smoothly. If it didn't he was irritated. In his family, where tempers flew easily and where shouting matches were as common as the row of worn-out sneakers by the door, Terry's stubborn single-mindedness was tolerated, but grudgingly.

Rika, who spent much of her free time at the Fox household, often welcomed Terry home after his first run of the day. She, too, felt his wrath often. She said he always purposely left his bloodied leg on for three or four hours before going out for the second run. His mother tried to warn him that he risked infection, but he didn't listen and refused to discuss his pain.

Perhaps no one can ever know the strain Terry felt during those days. No one could ever really understand how tough he had to make himself to run when every human instinct told him to stop and care for his injuries. Betty saw more of his suffering than anyone else in the family, but she could not relieve him of his burden. It became almost impossible for her to watch her son run.

One of Terry's secrets was that he set small goals for himself. He didn't think about running ten miles in the morning. Instead he ran one mile at a time. "I broke it down. Get that mile down, get to that sign, get past that corner and around that bend. That's all it was. That's all I thought about. I didn't think of anything else."

Terry's route took him through Ioco, the company town built for employees of the Imperial Oil refinery. He ran past cozy, middle-class homes with wooden siding and car ports, past Burrard Inlet and the smoke of the refinery; he ran up hills – some of which seemed to have come straight from the palettes of A.Y. Jackson or Tom Thomson – to Sasamat Lake, which is the same deep blue-green as the mountains reflected in its water. The weather was continually damp. Moss crawled over graffiti on the rocks, and the telephone wires always sparkled with rain drops.

To help him forget the agony in his stump and foot, Terry would count telephone poles and play mathematical games about how far he'd come and how far he had yet to go. Whenever he saw someone walking ahead of him, he sped up to pass them with a flourish. If he was going to run, he was going to run with style and speed.

"People helped me. People got to know me on the run. I'd say hi to them as I got to know them, especially the people in Ioco. I got to know mailmen and milkmen. I got to know all the truck drivers on that ten-mile route."

He remembered the tiny elderly lady in the blue coat and fur collar whom he passed nearly every day. She was painfully slow herself, but they always exchanged a cheery word. Sometimes, though, he had the greatest effect on those he never met. One woman who had watched him run wrote this letter:

In January 1979, we moved to Port Moody and I started a 6:30 A.M. routine driving our little dog to a deserted area along the newly constructed road, the extension of Ioco east, to let him have his run. This is when I first saw you "in training" and simply could not believe my eyes. Even though I am in good health and have two good legs, there I was driving the car. You shamed me into buying a warm-up suit and jogging shoes. Unfortunately, jogging to me is the most tortuous form of exercise.

My routine didn't last too long. But there you were, morning after morning in sleet and snow and cold rain keeping up a continuous arduous pace – wearing shorts while I shivered driving along beside our dog.

During those first months, Terry, there was so much agony in your face, but so much determination, too. I wanted to stop and say how much [my son] Michael and I admired your effort. I was so overwhelmed it may have created embarrassment for you. . . .

Through the summer I saw you several times, sweat pouring down your face. One very hot day, I wanted to stop to offer a ride, get a cool drink, anything to get you out of the heat. Once I circled the area three times just to make sure you were going to make it along that lone deserted stretch of road.

In late summer and fall we missed seeing you somehow, so when you suddenly appeared again we could see the tremendous improvements. Your leg was almost twice the size, very muscular and strong. Your whole body looked stronger and you moved easier without showing stress and pain. Indeed you looked very happy, justifiably pleased with your progress.

(Signed) Shelagh and Michael

On his ten- and fifteen-mile runs, Terry looked on that stretch of road as a proprietor would. "It was my ten miles. I knew it better than anybody. I knew every niche and crack in the road. You couldn't find a better ten miles in the world."

There were days, of course, that he wanted to give up and nearly did. He suffered bouts of diarrhoea and shivered with cold sweats. Along the sea-wall at Stanley Park, he'd buck the wind. The next day would be bright and sunny, and his resilient body would sing with speed and energy. It was always changing. One day just before Christmas, when he had gone only half a mile, the lower half of his artificial leg broke in two, sending him sprawling on the pavement. He gathered his dignity and picked up his leg and, holding the parts in his hand, hitchhiked home. Then he clamped the leg together and set out to run another five miles.

Three days later he wrote in his diary: *Christmas Day, day of rest.* He had run 101 days in a row and stopped only on Christmas Day to please his mother, who had asked him to skip that day for her sake.

In January, Terry missed his three-month appointment for a chest X-ray at the cancer clinic. "I just didn't think I needed it. I was really, really busy. Almost always if the cancer spreads it spreads in the first six or nine months. I really did not believe the cancer would come back."

Terry hated the X-rays. "Everytime I went down, I was shivering and it wasn't because I was cold. I was afraid."

Certain that he had been cured, Terry directed every thought, every action to his running. He had asked Rika to join him on the run. Although still loyal to him, Rika hesitated because she found herself going home in tears too many nights. It was apparent their chaste romance had withered. Confused, Rika asked for help from the pastor at her church. He advised her not to go on the run because, although she and Terry knew the limits of their relationship, not everyone would understand. Living in such close quarters with two men would lessen her credibility as a Christian, she was told.

And just a few months before they were scheduled to leave, Doug started having second thoughts. He was prone to introversion and self-doubt, and felt he couldn't offer Terry the support and help he would need on the long run. He tried to back down. But Terry wanted him, and Doug's parents thought the trip would help him learn to be comfortable with more people.

"One thing about Doug," Terry said, "I knew I could depend on him. When he gave his word, you knew he would stick by it. I knew he was somebody who would not give up. We'd been friends for a long, long time. He knew a lot about running techniques and injuries. He knew a whole lot about the whole run. He could stand a long situation without things changing and I knew that. I thought we could get along well together for a long time. I thought the trip would help him a lot."

Soon the plans and dreams started taking shape. Ford had agreed to supply a camper van, which Doug would drive. Adidas came through with running shoes for both Doug and Terry. Imperial Oil offered $500 in gas money and Canada Safeway donated $500 cash and food vouchers. Pacific Western Airlines offered transportation to Winnipeg, and private donors paid their way on Air Canada to St. John's. Labatt's Brewery donated beer for a dance the Fox family organized at the Port Coquitlam Recreation Centre, which raised $2,500 to help pay for living expenses along the way. War Amputations of Canada offered to repair and replace Terry's prosthesis.

A tentative itinerary was made up, with St. John's as the starting point. If Terry left there on April 12 and ran thirty miles daily – despite the fact that his best at-home effort was twenty-three miles a day – he would arrive at Port Renfrew on the west coast of Vancouver Island September 10.

The national office of the Canadian Cancer Society agreed to promote the run, although organizers were still sceptical of its success. Terry's run would come hot on the heels of the society's busy spring fund-raising season, and they worried that the volunteers, who would be suffering from post-campaign fatigue, would not rally again behind the Cancer Society caduceus.

Terry now had the go signal from every quarter, even if some were reluctant to give it. All that he lacked was a medical certificate from a heart specialist saying that he was in sufficiently good health to attempt the run. That request came from Dr. Robert Macbeth, executive vice-president of both the Cancer Society and the National Cancer Institute, the society's research arm.

That last hurdle was perhaps the most difficult. One week before Terry was to board a plane for St. John's, he saw Dr. Akbar Lalani, a New Westminster heart specialist. Terry had already decided that, no matter what the doctor said, he was going to run. But he also knew he had developed a condition known among athletes as an enlarged heart and among specialists as left ventricular hypertrophy. Terry's condition was slightly different from the condition commonly associated with athletes because only the left ventricle, not his whole heart, was enlarged.

Doctors are still not sure whether Terry's condition was related to use of the drug adriamycin during chemotherapy, whether it was merely an athletic condition, or whether it was the result of a congenital malformation. Terry, however, believed the problem resulted from the drug treatment.

After Dr. Lalani examined Terry, "He told me, 'Something could go wrong with you tomorrow, yet you're in the top physical shape. Right now you're doing all this activity, your heart's taking it, but you might die tomorrow because of it. But what will probably happen is that you'll live to be seventy years old.' It was abnormal but it wasn't really threatening at the time. He couldn't say whether something would happen or not. So I was sitting there. I didn't know whether the condition was going to affect me or not.

"He said to me, 'Why don't you run across B.C. first?' But I had already run more than 3,000 miles proving myself. Why run across B.C. first?"

Lalani found Terry "agitated" and understandably very keen to start his run. He knew that Terry would run with or without his sanction. He gave it reluctantly.

He warned Terry that if he felt he was experiencing any problems with his heart he should stop running, immediately. Lalani cautioned him to beware of dizzy spells, shortness of breath, and rapid tiring. He suggested that Terry had set himself too great a task by hoping to run up to forty miles a day. He said ten miles daily was safer.

Terry must have blanched when he heard the symptoms

associated with heart failure. He had experienced them already. He had told no one but Rika, whom he had sworn to secrecy. Terry had thought the dizziness and double vision he had felt while running were connected with the heat.

Just before he left for St. John's he felt those symptoms again. "I worried that maybe there was something wrong. I was afraid. But I just kept going because they went away. So I figured I was okay. After all, I was doing what I wanted, what I felt I had to do and had worked so hard for and dreamed of doing. It wasn't going to be easy; it was going to be hard. But I was going to do it and that's all there was to it."

Stubborn, sometimes so obsessed with his dream that he became one-dimensional, Terry never considered that he was risking his life to pay back his debt and prove that he was not disabled. "I was paying the price all the time. If I was running up Burnaby Mountain I was paying the price right there. The pain and the fatigue, the work and the hours, the *hours* I put into it every day. My life went around my running."

Terry had little time for reflection, or even for running, in the last days before leaving home, although he was still writing notes in his diary exhorting himself to run every day. But he was busy with all the details that accompany preparations for a long trip, along with local radio, television, and newspaper interviews. He was already used to interviewers since, as an amputee who was an accomplished athlete, he had always drawn some media attention and had been the subject of several feature stories. Among those most loyal to Terry early and consistently in his hometown were CJOR radio, CKVU television's evening interview program "The Vancouver Show," and the *Columbian*, the New Westminster daily newspaper.

By the end of the first week in April, the preparations for the run were completed. Doug and Terry were ready to leave. There was a little crowd at the airport, which included Rika, Doug's parents, Betty, Rolly, Darrell, Judith, Fred and his girlfriend Theresa, Blair MacKenzie and his two daughters, and Harry Crawshaw and his wife. Harry was the octogenarain who claimed to have set a new record cycling across Canada for the Cancer Society.

Terry shook hands with everyone, including Rika, who felt the least she deserved was a kiss. Then he hugged his dad and Judith, who was crying, and last of all his mother, who was weeping. He held on to her for the longest time, tried manfully to hold back his own tears, but finally let a few tumble down. It was difficult for him to leave, not knowing what lay on the road ahead.

As he and Doug strapped themselves into their seats at the front of the Pacific Western Airlines 737, Terry looked up in surprise to see the smiling face of a BCTV reporter with a microphone in her hand. Was she going with them? Not at all, it was just the farewell interview.

The journey to Terry's land of Oz had begun in a swirl of camera lights, a chorus of good-byes and the roar of jet engines. He could never haved dreamed it then, but when he returned to British Columbia soil he would not be just a hometown hero, he would be the pride of a nation.

He had a magnificent accomplishment behind him. He had run 3,159½ miles in training. Those first 3,000 he ran to prepare himself. The next 5,300 would be for everyone else.

# Chapter Six

Terry saw his country as few had ever seen it before. Canadians opened their doors to share their warm-hearted hospitality with him. Images of people he'd met and places he'd visited stayed sharp and clear in Terry's mind:

"I remember going through Gander and seeing kids playing road hockey. Where are those kids now? Are they still playing road hockey? Are they playing in a rink? I think about that, all across Canada. What are people doing in the little towns, the people that I met?"

His diary captures the homely essence of the first months of his Marathon of Hope, Terry's great adventure:

## NEWFOUNDLAND

*April 18, Port Blandford, Newfoundland*
*140 miles*

*As we were passing through Port Blandford, Mr. Roland Greening drove by me and told me to come to his store when I was finished. I took a fifteen-minute break and took off again. I was very, very tired and could only manage another two miles. We got just inside the Terra Nova National Park. Back at Mr. Greening's store, Mrs. Greening directed us to the house, which was a beautiful old home right beside the ocean. Here I had a bath and made my phone calls. We learned that Mr. Greening had cancer in his thyroid two years ago. The fish they made was cod and it was just fantastic, a cheese cod soufflé.*

After we ate our meal, these girls, two of them, came over
to the house and asked if they could see us. They were about
fifteen, I think. They were shy. They sat down and didn't say
anything. Finally I started talking to them and asking them
about their school. Then they started asking me a few things.
Before they left, they asked me to come over. I said I would
and they both asked if they could have a kiss, so I kissed
them both and then they went away.

About half an hour later, about ten girls came over – those
two girls had come back with eight more – and they were all
shy again. It was fantastic. I showed them my leg, and how it
works, and we joked about not having to change my socks. It
was a really warm time. Doug really liked it, too. Then they
weren't so shy any more. They became open and I had one of
the best times I've ever had. If I could have done that every
night it would have been relaxing.

You know, we all became friends, all these little fifteen-
year-old girls. When they left, they all did the same thing.
They kissed me.

*April 19, Glovertown, Newfoundland*
*165 miles*

During my rest period Caleb Ackerman met us. I had an
hour's rest and then did another four miles. Those miles were
tough until Mr. Ackerman, with his Newfoundland and
Canadian flags, came up behind me in his car. Then I breezed
through my final couple of miles. We made it just outside the
Terra Nova Park. Here I got in the car with Caleb, and he
drove us through Glovertown, a-honkin' his horn. We went
to a gym where girls were playing basketball. There I was
very unprepared to speak, but I told everyone what I was
doing and we collected over $100. Caleb phoned ahead to try
and increase receptions for us in towns ahead.

*April 20, Gambo, Newfoundland*
*190 miles*

I find the downhills very jarring on my body. Along the way,
two ladies from Clarenville stopped by on their way to
Gander, where they were dropping off a lady going to

Scotland. They gave me a beautiful old cross as a friendly gesture. I find many people taking my photograph. . . . Then we drove ten miles back to Gambo where we met Gus Barrow. He drove us to the fire hall, where practically the whole town was waiting. It was really beautiful. The mayors of Glovertown and Gambo introduced me and then I talked to the crowd. In fifteen minutes we raised more than $700 in a town with less than 3,000 people. It was a fantastic feeling and a day I will never forget because I hope it is a start of things to come.

*April 21, Gander, Newfoundland*
*215 miles*

It was an exciting day in Gambo. People came and lined up and gave me ten, twenty bucks just like that. And that's when I knew that the run had unlimited potential. I started to try to do whatever I could to let the Cancer Society know about that potential. I needed them. I tried to let them know as best I could that I was dependent on them to have things prepared and set up before I got there. In some places they did it; in some places, they didn't. It was frustrating for me because I knew there was not only money not being raised but people who I could have inspired, people who could have learned something, were missing me and that was because of the Cancer Society. But in Newfoundland, considering that I was just starting and they had no idea, they didn't know how people were going to respond, just as I didn't. All in all, I'm happy with the Newfoundland Cancer Society. They tried. Theirs is not a wealthy province, and they were the very first one.

We drove to Gander city hall where there were three people waiting for us, including the mayor. It was a great disappointment considering the day before in Gambo. We talked to reporters for an hour and then came back to the hotel. I went for a beautiful drive.

*April 25, Springdale, Newfoundland*
*312 miles*

Sometimes I put on tapes of Hank Williams or Johnny Cash

and I'd drive and try and find the ocean. I liked the ocean, but not only that: I liked to drive away, just for the fact of driving, being free and relaxing and listening to music. I remember that free hour when I could just roam. I'd think, Here I am in Newfoundland, in Gander.

Our privacy is starting to be invaded and we can't get anything done. I am happy with the fund-raising, but upset that we don't have time to talk and meet people. At night, quite often, people were looking at the van and snooping around. Today the valve system on my leg had completely eroded away and was making a farting noise with every step. I got many sores from this so I had to convert over to my spare leg.

*April 26, South Brook Junction, Newfoundland*
*Day 15, 337 miles*

Today we got up at 4.00 A.M. As usual, it was tough. We drove the thirty-five miles back to the starting point and I took off again. This time I had the other leg with the ordinary knee. I had to consider at the start whether it would be effective. It was foggy this morning so I ran on the left side of the road. We wanted to cover fourteen miles right away because there was going to be a reception at the South Brook Junction. I was feeling pretty good and the first two and three-quarters miles went quite nicely. Then, all of a sudden, I was seeing eight pictures of everything. I was dizzy and light-headed, but I made it to the van. It was a frightening experience. Was it all over? Was everything finished? Would I let everybody down? Slowly the seeing double went away but my eyes were glassy and I was still light-headed. I told myself it is too late to give up. I would keep going no matter what happened. If I died, I would die happy because I was doing what I wanted to do. How many people could or can say that? I went out and did fifteen push-ups in the road and took off. My head was light but the double-sightedness went away. At five miles Doug and I talked about it for a while. I cried because I knew I was going to make it or be in a hospital bed or dead. I want to set an example that will never be forgotten. It is courage and not foolishness. It isn't a waste.

*April 29, Deer Lake, Newfoundland*
*412 miles*

*It was another one of those days when nothing was organized*
*so we raised very little money. Nobody came to meet us in a*
*town of 5,500. I took another break during which I phoned*
*the local schools to let them know I would be coming back*
*tomorrow. Then I did another three miles. I would have liked*
*to have done more but I was drained and we had to meet the*
*mayor at 5 P.M. We were given a room at the Deer Lake*
*Hotel and a free meal. After this I showered and made my*
*umpteenth million phone call. I called Ron Calhoun [special*
*events chairman of the Cancer Society] and had a good*
*conversation. Things will be better from now on, I hope.*

When Terry was halfway across Newfoundland, Dr. Robert
Macbeth of the National Cancer Institute received the report on
Terry's heart. He was worried and arranged a medical examination
for Terry in Corner Brook. Terry was told of the appointment, but
skipped it.

*May 1, Corner Brook, Newfoundland*
*465 miles*

*One Roman Catholic School I will never forget. They sang a*
*song to receive me. Part of the words were: "Thank you,*
*Lord, for giving us Terry." It was beautiful, it really brought*
*tears to my eyes.*

Terry didn't know at the time, but the children of All Hallow
School donated all their recess money to the Marathon of Hope.
He told the children: "I bet some of you feel sorry for me. Well,
don't. Having an artificial leg has its advantages. I've broken my
right knee several times and it doesn't hurt a bit."

*May 3, St. George's Junction, Newfoundland*
*515 miles*

*I got in the fire truck with a Mr. Tim Conway, who had*
*done a wonderful job in setting everything up. Near the town*
*I got out and walked to the fire hall. The local cadets walked*
*behind me and so did a lot of the townspeople. They played*

"When the Saints Go Marching In." It was a magnificent feeling. I was really stirred. I raised about $800. Everyone wanted my autograph and a kiss. The reception really picked me up. Then we ate a cold meal and a warm meal at a nearby restaurant and another meal at a gas station. This last one was the first meal we have had to pay for. Then we drove to a hide-out and I did my postcards and went to bed.

May 4, past St. George's on Highway 1
521 miles

Today at 4:30 A.M., I couldn't get out of bed. I was sick and my stomach was in knots. I lay there and later Doug drove to the starting point. We had a big argument, so we drove back to a place off the highway and I slept again. But I never got better. I finally tried to run. It was snowing and miserable, and I had a huge hill to go up. I couldn't even manage a hundred yards without standing to hold my stomach and catch my breath. I managed three miles and then crawled into the van. I cried so hard and felt so weak. I changed and slept. I think the problem was something we ate last night.

Later I had some tomato soup and hot chocolate. Then I went to bed. When I woke up I made myself some cake and had some oranges and some milk. My stomach was still upset and I was a bit weak, but I felt a bit better.

May 5, on the road to Port aux Basques
548 miles

Today the terrain was up and down. We are passing through a mountain range. We learned today they had already collected more than $8,000 in Port aux Basques. Fantastic. I really want to make Port aux Basques tomorrow because they have got everything planned, but I am worried that I might not be strong enough to make it. We stayed at the Starlight Hotel where we were given our meal and lodging. I had a real good shower here. Then I drove to the ocean. Newfoundland has two things, the ocean and people. There is really no scenery or vegetation here.

The next day, the citizens of Port aux Basques, a town with a population of 10,000, raised another $2,000, making their total contribution $10,000, equal to one dollar per person.

Despite the excitement, optimism and comparative freedom of the first months, at times there was an undercurrent of tension between Terry and Doug. Doug sometimes became uncommunicative, and Terry frustrated. Both were stubborn.

"I know I did stuff I shouldn't have," Doug said. "Terry wanted me to make phone calls to arrange publicity and give interviews. I thought he should have made the phone calls. For one thing, nobody wanted to talk to me, they wanted to talk to Terry Fox. If you're calling B.C. from Newfoundland, you might as well put Terry Fox on the line.

"After a while I didn't want to do anything for him, just drive the van, which wasn't nice of me. I think I went too far with pride and rebellion. It wasn't the Christian thing to do. You know sometimes when you do things that they're wrong, but you do them anyhow.

"We'd still be talking but the tension was really bad. Twice I refused to mark miles for him. At Kelly's Mountain, Nova Scotia, he had to throw rocks at the van to get my attention because I was always reading. It was my job to stand by the van at the end of each mile and have water ready for him. Sometimes I would just stretch out my hand to give him his water and neither of us would say a word. Once when I handed him water he just threw it in my face.

"At Grand Falls and Bishop's Falls he agreed to speak to three high schools. The next day he was pissed off and didn't want to do it. I couldn't figure out why he was so mad. There seemed to be a double side. Sometimes he didn't seem to give a damn about other people; at other times he gave an incredible damn. It took me three months to figure out how tough it was. Tougher than any of us could ever know.

"Sometimes I wondered how much was obsession and how much was devotion. After a while I saw there was more devotion than I had figured. It was a fine line he had to balance between keeping in the public eye, keeping the Cancer Society happy, keeping me happy, and accomplishing the run.

"Sometimes he'd bitch at me about a mile marker that it seemed like a long one. Once it was. The mile ended in the middle of a hill and there was no where to pull over so I went to the top of a hill and he had to run an extra three-quarters of a mile. Boy, was he mad!

"In Newfoundland I told him I couldn't care less whether he made it or not. Of course, I didn't mean it. But he just made me so mad."

## NOVA SCOTIA

*May 7, North Sydney, Nova Scotia*
*579 miles*

*After Newfoundland, it should have been clear sailing for fund-raising because I phoned the national office and I phoned Nova Scotia and told them, "You've got a lot of potential. Use me." But Nova Scotia did not. We made more money in Newfoundland than we did in Nova Scotia. When I got to Sydney, Nova Scotia, there were two or three people from the Cancer Society waiting for us, and Sydney's a pretty big place. That was pretty upsetting because I'd made it all the way across Newfoundland and now I've made it to Nova Scotia, things were picking up, $10,000 in the little tiny town of Port aux Basques and here we are in big Sydney and there's nothing, absolutely nothing. Nobody even knew. It wasn't even in the media.*

*We decided we would go into town and try to get a bunch of media stuff going. We went to all the radio stations and did a lot of work. Since I hadn't slept all night because we had a rough crossing on the ferry from Newfoundland, I was already tired. Then the CBC wanted to film me running, so we decided that I would go out and run again.*

*The CBC was filming me from the side, right on the Trans Canada Highway. They were only going about five miles an hour when I heard this huge freight truck come barrelling up and not slowing down. Smack. At fifty miles per hour it hit the CBC vehicle, forcing it off the road, over a ditch and into the woods. One of the CBC men fell out the back onto the highway and rolled into the ditch. I thought he was dead. He was conscious but couldn't move. The other two guys were* hurt, but not seriously. The CBC truck was totalled and the camera equipment ruined. It was terrible. If I had been five yards farther ahead, I would have been killed. If the accident had occurred thirty yards before, the two in the truck would have gone down a big ravine. We went to see them in the hospital later. I couldn't run any more.

*May 10, Port Hawkesbury, Nova Scotia*
*660 miles*

The Cancer Society here in Nova Scotia is doing nothing and money is being wasted. I would love to get my hands on the people in Halifax. Bob McKeighan from the Ford dealership in Port Hawkesbury came and saw us. He was going to set things up and have dinner with us. He also got our clothes cleaned and the van vacuumed. He is very nice. So is his wife.

*May 14, on Highway 7*
*767 miles*

Twenty-six miles is now my daily minimum. It is beautiful, quiet, peaceful country. I love it. Very few dogs, so far. Few or no trucks. Very little traffic. I need this. It is nice not to have huge freight trucks ramming past me. I am now carrying my own water bottle when I run and making my own lunches. Doug won't do a thing for me. I saw four rabbits and a beaver today. Also one dead porcupine and two dead skunks. After running I drove up an old road to a big hill in the middle of nowhere. No one can find us here. A peaceful evening, finally. Got lots done. Postcards, shit container cleaned, etc. Made my supper. We were in a field on the top of a hill. Beautiful!

*May 15, Sheet Harbour, Nova Scotia*
*794 miles*

We parked in a beautiful location overlooking the sea. The ocean was much prettier today because of the sunshine. After my break I ran until a lady from the Cancer Society in Sheet Harbour came to see me. They had a reception set up for me at 5:00 and wanted me to run with the school kids. When I ran with the kids I really burned it just to show them how

*fast I could go. They were tired and puffing. All right! I met
quite a few people who had cancer. A great reception, finally,.
in Nova Scotia. Today I was feeling dizzy and light-headed
again.*

By mid-May, Terry was finally starting to feel the warm spring sun
on his back as he ran. His face was ruddy, wind-burned, and thin-
ner, highlighting his cheekbones. His body seemed frailer than
when he left, but he shooed aside comments about his weight, saying he had lost only seven pounds and most of that from his upper
torso, which had flowered magnificently during his months of
weight-lifting and was now reduced to humbler proportions.

In Port Coquitlam, Betty and Rolly were riveted to the 6:00 and
11:00 P.M. television news broadcasts, hoping for a glimpse of
their son. Although he called them collect every Thursday and was
effusive with optimism, they wanted to see him in the flesh to rest
their minds. They were worried by what they saw on television.
He seemed scrawny and worn out to Betty. Then Terry had called
from Sheet Harbour, Nova Scotia, in tears. He was sad and nearly
desperate: Doug had withdrawn completely and Terry could not
cope without help.

Betty and Rolly took a week's vacation and flew to Halifax to
see Terry and try to wrestle with the difficulties the boys were having. The negotiations took place in the home of a "nice little lady
who lived somewhere off Highway 7 in Nova Scotia. There was all
this swearing," Betty recalled, "and I would have been swearing,
too, if I wasn't in that lady's house!"

Betty and Rolly acted as model parents. Though it may have
been tempting to take Terry's side, they rose above parental
loyalties and stood squarely in the centre. They knew that Doug
was stubborn, just as Terry was. They knew that Terry was
demanding and that Doug tended to withdraw rather than con-
front. They encouraged Doug to express his feelings, and they
used the homely analogy of a couple of newlyweds who had to
learn to get along together in close quarters.

"If you have to yell, yell," Betty told Doug.

Terry later recalled of the meeting that "Mom and Dad really
helped because they straightened us out. They showed me how to
understand Doug's side more, and I think Doug saw my side more.
Just having them to talk to as a go-between was important and

good. You see, all along I never had anybody to talk to. When I was frustrated I was alone. Doug was somebody I couldn't talk to. We worked under pressure. I realized I was hurting him at times, that I was bitching too much at times. Doug realized that he could help me more, too."

Terry's true contrition came out in an emotional speech at the Dartmouth Vocational School a few days later.

*May 20, Dartmouth, Nova Scotia*
*916 miles*

*With my parents we took the ferry across the bay and met the Mayor of Dartmouth. Then I ran to the vocational school here with fifty students. I ran about a mile. They had raised about $3,000. What a great group of kids! Too bad not everybody was doing that. I did my speech and I couldn't help but cry when I said how Doug had to have courage to put up with and understand me when I'm tired and irritable. Then we drove back to Truro.*

*Had supper with my parents. A lady gave me a picture of her daughter and told me to phone her and that she liked me.*

[People] seem to forget what I am doing this for. They think I am running across Canada on some kind of ego trip. It is a personal challenge, but I'm trying to raise as much money as I can . . . I need their support.

Terry, quoted in the Halifax *Mail Star*, May 21, 1980

*May 22, Springhill, Nova Scotia*
*972 miles*

*It poured rain for the last two miles. Thunderstorm and lightning. My mom and dad came out for the last five miles. After that we drove to Springhill where we met Ron Jefferson, who had done a fantastic job organizing things here. I was in a bitchy mood, unfortunately. I wish I could relax more. Anyway, I ran another mile into city hall with fire engines and a police escort. There were a lot of people here to meet me. I did my speech and it went well and then I signed autographs. After that we went for a lobster dinner (great) with Ron and some other firemen and my parents. We* learned about the mine explosion here and that Anne Murray was from here. After that we came to a boarding house to sleep. They gave me some good advice. Be disappointed in the fund-raising, but not mad! I've got to try to control myself. My mom and dad left tonight for an early flight tomorrow morning.

## PRINCE EDWARD ISLAND

*May 24, Borden, Prince Edward Island*
*1028 miles*

*I made it perfectly for the 2:30 P.M. ferry across Northumberland Strait to Prince Edward Island. We met the captain on board and he spent about an hour with us. It was great. Then I ran four and a quarter miles into Borden. It was a cute town. I had a very heavy wind in my face. Then we went to a motel where we met people from the Cancer Society in Charlottetown who are doing a fabulous job. I had a great shower and watched part of the sixth game of the Stanley Cup play-offs between Philly and the New York Islanders. Then I drove to Summerside. It is beautiful country. I finally relaxed!*

*May 25, Highway 1 en route to Charlottetown*
*1,056 miles*

*Today I made it out of bed again. Boy, was it a beautiful morning. In terms of sun, weather, and terrain this was the most beautiful day so far. A guy from the local radio station was actually there at 5:00 in the morning when we took off. He covered us all day. What a tremendous support! The first twelve miles were relaxing. We parked right on the ocean, away from everything. Great!*

*When we went back out it was cloudy, windy, and cold. The next ten miles were okay. I was in some hilly areas, still beautiful. There were lots of people out to cheer me on and support me. Incredible! We collected over $600 on the road today, our best. We also learned that they now have $40,000 in Newfoundland.*

*I was very sore and tired. It is hard to even walk. I've got to get up and over the pain threshold. When I came out of the van after my rest I was weary, but there was a long line of cars and people to cheer me on so I made it. I had another dizzy spell during the run. Still freezing, but I wasn't wearing sweats so people could see my leg. I'd run just over twenty-eight miles.*

## May 26, Charlottetown, Prince Edward Island
## 1,074 miles

*I was scheduled to run into Charlottetown at 9:00 A.M. Therefore I got a chance to sleep in. It was great! We got up at 7:00 A.M. I did some postcards. We had to drive to a school where I talked to 900 kids. Boy, were they ever a happy group. Then I ran three miles into town. Along the way, two schools greeted me and cheered me on. Many people are congratulating me and I can't figure out what for.*

Early in the morning, Doug recalled, a little lady came out of her house and walked to the road to the Marathon of Hope van. She was wearing her nightgown and slippers and had a five-dollar bill in her hand. She asked if anybody wanted coffee, then went back into her house.

## NEW BRUNSWICK

*May 28, 28 miles, Moncton, New Brunswick*
*1,130 miles*

*The springs in my knee joint are worn away but I struggled and pounded out the twelve miles. I saw a moose. We went back to Shediac High School where I talked to about 900 students. They were all Acadians. I really enjoyed these people. Around five people fainted during the speech. It was very hard to believe! Then we went out to talk to more media and Stan Barker of the Cancer Society took my leg to Fredericton to get it repaired. I put on the other leg and it was worse. After a half mile I fell flat on my face. I couldn't*

*keep my balance and I was struggling to make ground again.
My foot and leg and back are all being overstressed to
compensate for the malfunctioning knee joint. I didn't think I
would make it twenty-eight miles, but I did and it was
fantastic when I made it. I couldn't believe I was looking at
the back of the van for the last time that day. We ran right
through the city of Moncton, down the main street, and
collected a lot of money. When one car would start to honk,
they all would! It was great.*

This next was the sort of day that frustrated Terry more than he
could express. The worst was having to drive a hundred miles
round trip back to Moncton to attend a press conference and a
fund-raising dinner after slogging twenty-nine miles through heat
and humidity. He hadn't slept the night before because of the high
temperatures; coming from the cool of British Columbia, he was
not used to the muggy atmosphere.

*May 29, 29 miles, Highway 2, west of Moncton, New
Brunswick, 1,159 miles*

*I was dead all morning for twelve miles. For the next ten
miles, the paved shoulder on the Trans Canada had a steep
slant and it is hard on my ankle. I took another break,
during which I made phone calls and then did my last seven
miles. We drove back fifty miles to Moncton and later we
drove fifty miles back to bed. We learned that St. John would
have nothing organized for us. I can't believe it.*

*We were advised to go directly on the Trans Canada #2
(and bypass St. John). I try so hard and then get let down. I
am going to run right down this city's main street. Doug is
going to follow behind and honk. We will be rebels, we will
stir up noise. People will know Terry Fox ran out of his way
to St. John for a reason!*

Terry's brother Darrell, who was seventeen at the time, skipped
his high-school graduation and joined the Marathon of Hope in St.
John to help his brother. The family hoped that Darrell, with his
sparky humour and generous good nature, would be a natural buf-
fer between Terry and Doug. By that time, however, Terry and

Doug were operating amicably. For Darrell, it was the start of the proudest three months of his life. He felt somehow connected with history in the making. His jokes and sly tricks may have clouded what was obvious – his insights and the fact that he simply adored his big brother.

*May 31, 29 miles, St. John, New Brunswick*
*1,217 miles*

*I was still sore all day. The first twelve miles were awful, especially the final three during which I was dead tired. Also pissed off that nothing was being done in St. John. Fortunately, the mayor, who is a heart-attack victim and a marathon runner, got a radio station behind me and the local paper. The next ten miles were better. Darrell arrived and it was very heart-warming to see him. Brought a few tears as we embraced. Got me moving a bit faster. We finished right in the middle of St. John.*

Cancer Society internal memo: Terry once again refused the medical in New Brunswick. His parents indicated that he was old enough to make his own decisions and they were not about to influence him.

Betty said it didn't happen that way. "What we said was that if we, as parents, had had any say, Terry never would have started," Betty recalled later.

Darrell was devoted to Terry and couldn't wait to swing into the rhythm of the Marathon. He was intensely loyal and was never heard to utter a word of criticism about his brother.

"By the time I got there," Darrell said, "things seemed okay between Terry and Doug. They seemed to have settled down. I didn't notice anything wrong. The first few days I just watched. I didn't know how things worked. I'd see how they did things and then I'd help.

"When I first saw Terry on the highway, he looked so lonely. Just to look at the road, to see it keep going, even each bend is so long. I don't know why, but I hugged him, I couldn't help myself.

"In the middle of St. John, the cars went by. People just looked at him in amazement. They'd just stare. They didn't know what was going on. I was mad when he ran through the city and there was nobody; to go out of his way and raise nothing, it was a complete waste of time. All that work for nothing.

"It seemed that Stan Barker of the Cancer Society was the only one doing anything.

"There were a lot of firsts for me. To be given free meals and to give interviews, all that was new. Then later, I saw the way Terry affected people. Once he was talking at a baseball game, everyone looked so interested and clapped for him, and the players came out to shake his hand. Sometimes it didn't seem like there was much to be done – just give Terry support, tell him how good he looked running.

*June 1, 23 miles, Highway 7, New Brunswick*
*1,240 miles*

*It's really good to have Darrell along. It was boiling hot and I got very tired and the miles went slowly. One idiot tried to drive me off the road. I took my break and tried again, but only managed one mile. I am very tired and sore. I need a break and I've got to take it. I'll turn failure to victory.*

*Goal: Home October 31st. Miles to go: 4,060 out of total 5,300. Twenty-eight miles a day! 145 running days to October 31st. 153 days left till October 31st. Therefore eight days to spare.*

*June 6, 30 miles, Bristol, New Brunswick*
*1,376 miles*

*Today it was a beautiful morning. No wind, sunny, and the sun coming up was great. Beautiful farmland. The first few miles were the usual torture. My foot was blistered bad, but my stump wasn't too bad. After twelve miles I found out we had to drive back to Hartland and meet the mayor. The mayor wasn't there so I went to a school and talked to a large group of kids. Then, exhausted, I slept. Today I had tremendous support. Everybody honked and waved. People all over looked out of their homes and stores and cheered me on.*

*June 7, 26 miles, Perth-Andover, New Brunswick*
*1,402 miles*

*I was in pain this morning and continually stopped to relieve the pressure. Slowly but surely twelve miles went by and left me just out of Perth-Andover. We parked in a beautiful grass field along the St. John River. On my mile twelve, a guy told me to look for a young bull moose in a pond, but I saw a deer. I slept very well while Doug and Darrell read on the river bank. Later in the town there was tremendous support and it quickened my pace right up for the remaining fourteen miles. I flew!*

In New Brunswick, Terry ran his all-time high of thirty miles per day. Doug recalled being worried when he got up to that mileage "because he had to run those miles, go to those receptions and there seemed no way he could do it. He was at his limit, absolutely all out all day. There was not a moment for him to relax."

In Edmundston, cheery, slightly plump Bill Vigars from the Ontario division of the Cancer Society joined the Marathon of Hope briefly to meet Terry, learn his schedule, and get them worked up for the big-top performance that awaited them in Ontario.

Doug, who was usually the first one up in the morning, remembered taking the gear out to the van at 4:30 A.M. There was Bill, sleeping in his car outside their hotel, having driven all night from Toronto. It was their first meeting.

"I was getting the van ready and this guy jumps out; he's just putting his shirt on. I couldn't believe this was the Bill Vigars I had been talking to on the phone. I expected a man with a suit and a tie, and here was chubby little Bill, about thirty, with glasses.

"He was talking about a Toronto Blue Jay baseball game, about meeting Darryl Sittler, Bobby Orr, what they were going to do. We had high expectations. I'd told Bill on the phone that our goal in Ontario was a million dollars. He'd sort of laughed, but he was really interested in getting things done. Bill really believed it would be big, ten million dollars anyway.

"It was high-class. They had everything organized, the centre of Canada, it looked like something great was going to happen. It was sort of like things were crawling along and had potential but needed somebody to get it going."

But first there was Quebec.

## QUEBEC

*June 10th, 30 miles, Notre-Dame-du-Lac, Quebec*
*1,482 miles*

*Today I felt quite good at the start; the only problem is my cysts are bothering me. The first nine miles took me to the Quebec-New Brunswick border. Here we said good-bye to Stan, Mr. Gordon, and also to Bill Vigars for a while. The wind picked up and was hard in my face. We learned that there would be very little done in Quebec. Apparently they can't speak English. Maybe they also don't get cancer.*

*June 11, 26 miles, Highway 185, Quebec*
*1,508 miles*

*We slept well last night. It was quite cold in the van. The wind howled again all day. Right in my face. It is very difficult constantly running into the wind. It zaps it right out of your body and head. The first twelve miles were good and bad, off and on. Very hilly country all day. Lots of forest. All forest! My stump is still constantly giving me trouble. We parked down by a lake. All alone in the woods. Can't wash or shave or get a haircut. The only people here who know about the run are the truckers and the out-of-province people. Everyone else wants to stop and give me a lift.*

*June 12, 27 miles, Andreville, Quebec*
*1,535 miles*

*The St. Lawrence River is beautiful, so large. This is the best scenery we have had. The towns are simply gorgeous. We made it to St. Andre (Andreville). Here we phoned and camped behind the school for the night.*

None of the trio of west-coast boys could speak French. Doug made this fractured attempt at communicating: *Je ne parler pas français.* The others had mastered *oui* and *non* fairly well, but when it came to the intricacies of buying food (bags of marsh-mallows, doughnuts, tins of spaghetti and beef stew), they could only point and hope they were understood. When it came to asking for a shower, the three were completely lost, so they did without. "I felt like an idiot, an alien from another planet," Doug recalled, "so we went four or five days without a wash."

*Friday, June 13, 24 miles, Highway 20, Quebec*
*1,559 miles*

*The wind is simply howling and shaking. It is terrible. No way could I run against it, so I had to run behind the van. It was hard on Doug trying to stay a distance away. Terrible, ugly day. Somehow we turned zero miles into twenty-four. I got sick from the exhaust fumes of the van. I was given a beautiful shower and I was so dirty. Felt good!*

Darrell, in the back of the van, sat with his left leg stretched out full to keep the one side of the door open and his right arm stretched the other way to keep the right door open. The tape deck was turned on high, and the nostalgic sound of "American Graffiti" poured onto the highway. "I'd look into Terry's eyes," he recalled. "It was like he was looking at nothing, like he was chasing the van, like he was going to hop on for a ride. It hurt having to watch him, suffering. He'd run by a pole and I'd watch it get farther and farther away, then another would take its place. He wouldn't look at me so I'd watch his face a lot. He had to wear a jacket, the wind was blowing so hard. I watched it blowing his curls back from his face."

*June 15, 26 miles, Highway 20, Quebec*
*1,611 miles*

*I am tired and weary because people are continually forcing me off the road. I was actually honked off once. People are passing from behind me on this narrow road. It is so frustrating. They all drive at eighty miles per hour and don't slow down for anything. It is wearisome. Mental breakdown. We talked and ate with John Simpson and Scott Hamilton [who made the Cancer Society-sponsored documentary film of the marathon I Had a Dream] and then I did a long interview. In bed late again.*

There were highlights for Terry in Quebec, though they seem to have been more aesthetic than personal. He was charmed by the statuary around the churches, the beautiful cobbled streets of old Quebec City, and the tidy, antiquated shops. He admired the rolling battlefield at the Plains of Abraham, and there was the sheer fun of eating in a restaurant named the Marie Antoinette, the honour of meeting Gerard Côte, four-time Boston Marathon winner (1940, 1942, 1943, and 1948), and the excitement of being featured on the front page of the French language daily, *Le Soleil*. He believed if the Marathon had been better publicized, Quebeckers would have responded as other Canadians had.

However, Terry's overall impressions of *la belle province* were not favourable: "It was very disappointing; it's not because they're French and we're English. Anyone can get cancer. I'm running across Canada, and Quebec is a province in Canada. With me, it isn't a political or racial thing, it's just a human thing. Cancer can strike anybody. I'm trying to help out everybody in my run."

Terry was hurt and disappointed by the lack of response to his efforts. "In one stretch of Quebec, we collected thirty-five dollars while I ran 100 miles." Nor was he helped by the attitude of motorists and the police: "Near Quebec City I kept nearly getting hit because they drove so fast. Afterwards I decided I had to move over to the freeway, which had a side lane. It was perfectly safe and nobody was near me. I ran there for two days when the Quebec Provincial Police told me I couldn't run on it any more because it wasn't safe [and because of the traffic expected for the St. Jean Baptiste holiday weekend]. I had to get back on these other side roads. In Drummondville I got back on the little roads and kept nearly getting hit again. These cars were just whizzing by and shooing me off the road."

Then Terry was told that he would have to cool his heels for two days in Montreal so as to arrive in Ontario, especially Ottawa and Toronto, according to the schedule set up by Bill Vigars and the Ontario division of the Cancer Society. He agreed only when Bill told him the difference it might mean in fund-raising.

Terry ran into Montreal on a Sunday, using a route he had chosen and mapped out himself. He was accompanied by four wheelchair athletes and former Montreal Alouette kicker Don Sweet. As he and the others passed down the quiet morning streets, there were few passersby to cheer him on. He was running to the luxury of the Four Seasons Hotel, where the Marathon would be pampered as guests of the international hotel chain's president, Isadore Sharp. Sharp, who was a devoted philanthropist, had lost a teenage son to cancer. Along with some of his business partners, including Eddie Creed, he decided to tackle the corporate community to raise money for the Marathon of Hope.

Terry, Doug, and Darrell didn't quite know what to make of the posh surroundings, although Terry stood under a shower for an hour – or so he said. "I'm not used to seeing luxurious things," Darrell said later. "Our laundry bill was eighty dollars. Our T-shirts came back from the cleaners with paper around them, like when you buy them brand new!" Darrell was very proud of those shirts, anyway, because his name was emblazoned across the back identifying him as Terry's brother.

One night while Darrell was collapsed in front of a malfunctioning television set, Bev Norris, a Four Seasons publicist, walked in the room. She watched in amazement as Darrell pounded the set, presumably to improve its picture.

"Darrell Fox," Bev said in a mock, schoolteacherish tone, "do you realize you're staying in a hundred-dollar-a-night room?"

"How much would it cost if the T.V. worked?" Darrell shot back, grinning from ear to ear.

On June 23, Terry took the day off, and for the first time in seventy-three days of running, he wrote *zero* beside the mileage he recorded daily in his diary.

Terry was meant to relax in Montreal. He did his best but it was difficult for him. He didn't like sitting around; it made him edgy, he told the *Toronto Star* in one of his weekly interviews. In fact, relaxation didn't vitalize him, but made him only more anxious to run. He tried to have a good time. He spent some time with his old high-school buddy Clay Gamble, visited his Uncle Brian, took the subway to see the Olympic Stadium, and watched the Canadian Open Golf Tournament.

But what he really wanted to do was run. Doug believed that changing the pace undermined Terry psychologically and threw him off his rhythm.

On June 28, he was on the road again, dodging cars that zoomed past him at furious speeds. He ran much of the day looking over his shoulder. The temperature soared to 32°C. The boys on the Marathon started counting the days until they could leave Quebec and the isolation caused by their language difficulties.

# Chapter Seven

## ONTARIO

Back in early April, Terry had not been big news, particularly in Ontario. He had his west-coast supporters, but central Canada had yet to hear about him.

At that time, a story about a one-legged runner crossing Canada hadn't gone over well in the *Toronto Star*'s weekly feature meeting, but it had stuck in the mind of my boss, Bonnie Cornell. She'd watched Terry dipping his leg in the Atlantic on television and felt the paper should support him. Cancer was on her mind, too; her mother had died recently of the disease in her liver. With the luck of the assignment pool, she gave me the story on condition that the runner was credible.

The *Toronto Star*'s telephone operators may have voices like honey, but their minds are like detectives' and they enjoy nothing more than a challenge. When I asked them to find a one-legged runner somewhere in Newfoundland, they did. By mid-afternoon the call came through: "We have Mr. Terry Fox on the line."

Terry was in the home of the mayor of Come-By-Chance, Newfoundland. As Terry told me his story, his voice sounded young, a bit thick at times, as though a pebble had strayed to the roof of his mouth. I was captured immediately by his sincerity and matter-of-fact courage. What he had to say – about cancer, about his dreams of running 5,300 miles and fund-raising, about how he wasn't disabled – was unbelievable, yet he said it in such an ordinary, understated way, it enhanced his credibility.

Terry agreed to phone me every week until he reached British Columbia. British Columbia? He was barely into Newfoundland, had run only ninety-two miles and already I was starting to think as he did and vowed to be among the pack of well-wishers when he waded into English Bay in Vancouver.

I don't know which of us was more excited, Terry knowing that a big paper was interested in him and wanted a weekly progress report, or me, knowing I landed a good story.

With each weekly report came wisecracks from the newsroom: "How much longer is he going to hopping be across Canada?" "No one ever reads this, you know. It's boring." "It won't be news as long as he runs, it'll only be news when he stops." Of course, by the time he was front-page news, Terry had captured the interest of all those cynics.

We built a trust during those early telephone interviews and our chats became the highlights of my week. I was disappointed if he was too busy to do the interview himself. When Doug told me that sometimes I seemed too depressed, too worried on the telephone and that Terry liked people to be buoyant and positive, I tried to change my tone.

He told me about his dreams of ending the run in Stanley Park and how he would raise his arms and dance in the waves, saying to himself, "I did it. I did it!"

Once he told me of the ecstatic heights he reached while running, when his concentration and stride were in harmony and the pain dissolved into the rhythm of his motion: "When I'm really tired, I'm actually crying on the road. I get so emotional, but being in that state keeps me going."

Another day he read part of a poem that was given him by a Nova Scotia admirer named Mrs. Fox. He kept the poem tacked on the van's wall and he read it every night before bed. Here's one verse:

There are thousands to tell you it cannot be done,
There are thousands to prophesy failure;
There are thousands to point out to you one by one,
The dangers that wait to assail you.
But just buckle in with a bit of a grin,
Just take off your coat and go to it;
Just start in to sing as you tackle the thing
That "cannot be done," and you'll do it.
                    "It Couldn't Be Done," Edgar Albert Guest

Sometimes I'd share bits of news that Terry hadn't heard yet – that a song called "Run, Terry, Run," written by Vern Kennedy, had been recorded in his honour with all royalties going to the Cancer Society, that an anonymous Toronto woman had donated $5,000, and the big news – that the Four Seasons Hotel had challenged 999 companies to sponsor Terry at two dollars a mile.

We didn't meet until the last Saturday in June, when the *Star* sent me to Hawkesbury, a francophone town on the edge of the Ottawa River, to cover Terry's arrival in Ontario.

The flashing lights of the van and a police cruiser alerted me to Terry's arrival on the Quebec side of the Perley Bridge. Terry was running to the Ontario side, while I was driving, with an Ottawa photographer, toward him on the Quebec side. Then I saw him. His teeth were gritted together, and his face was a grimace, not so much of pain as of concentration. At times he'd suck in his lower lip, as though biting it. It was the same look children have when they struggle with a difficult math question. His eyes were closed, perhaps to the glare, perhaps to the distractions on the roadside.

As I drove by, I waved and surprised myself with a yelp, like that of a cheerleader: "Go, Terry!" He didn't look at me but just shot his hand up in a hasty acknowledgement. His attention was fixed on the road, and he lurched ahead, his whole body rocking with the swing of his artificial leg. I had expected a huskier, perhaps more manly type of athlete. Although he was five feet ten inches, he seemed smaller, certainly smaller than his news photographs had shown him, and therefore more childlike. The road seemed endless, his task impossible, and I gasped the way thousands of others had when they first saw Terry. I know that I didn't feel pity; instead I felt a great surge of emotion, admiration and, surprisingly, an uplift. Just as the man in Newfoundland had said, he made you feel good. Just as an Ontario woman said, he made you believe in the human race again.

Back on the Ontario side of the bridge there was a flurry of excitement. A crowd had formed in front of a little community centre, not far from the ballfield and the river. A couple of station wagons were parked on the grass, and were filled with printed ballons that read: WELCOME, TERRY. YOU CAN DO IT.

A brass band uncertainly rehearsed a melody that had a mind of its own. At last Terry was in sight. He was flanked by flag-bearers, a couple of men in jogging shorts. The youthful musicians gathered their courage and their instruments and burst, off key, into "Georgie Girl." The doors of the stations wagons were flung open, and thousands of balloons drifted skyward. The crowd, perhaps 200 or more, spontaneously shouted, "Hip, hip hooray" three times.

We all felt very pleased with that show of emotion and watched as a very sweaty Terry walked up the steps of the centre and shook hands with important people there. The local MPP, Albert Belanger, representing Ontario's Premier Bill Davis, started the ceremonies, saying, "I hope this walk – excuse me, this *run* . . ." Terry smiled appreciatively, as he wiped the drops of sweat that gathered at his chin. He rested his hands on his hips, stood a little lop-sided, and probably thought, Walk, my foot! At least the man had enough savvy to correct his mistake.

Then Terry, the boy who would never take a university class that required an oral report, took the microphone and told his story. He spoke easily, simply saying, "It's certainly great to get to Ontario, I'll tell you that. I'm glad you all came out. It makes a difference." Then he spoke of cancer, saying nobody was immune to it, "nobody here, nobody in Hawkesbury." Then he thanked the Cancer Society – "they're taking a chance on me and I think it's going to work out."

As he spoke, the people of Hawkesbury, some of them fresh from the baseball diamond, most of them standing in family groups, stared at the grass. The little children, who'd snuck up front, squatted down and squinted at Terry, curious and watchful.

Then the band started up and Terry walked inside the community centre for a press conference. As local reporters gathered round him at a table, I stood to the side listening to the questions but mostly looking at Terry. He was attractive. His head was a flurry of damp brown curls, bleached white at the temples. His eyebrows had gone the same pale colour, and there were two patches of pink sunburn on his cheekbones. Freckles were out in full glory. His T-shirt announced, TERRY FOX, MARATHON OF HOPE, and there was a damp spot on his grey shorts – the only kind he would wear – from perspiration seeping from the valve in his artificial leg.

Somebody asked him if he was running to find himself. The

answer came back swiftly, almost defensively: "This isn't soul-searching. I'm not trying to find something. I've found what I want."

Outside, the little fellows from the peewee baseball team, Fournier Mets, were still milling around. They'd collected six dollars for Terry and had been tongue-tied at the presentation and now they wanted to watch him run some more.

Fourteen-year-old Charles Tittley was riding his bike across the grass, doing wheelies, until Terry came out. "I found that story of his very touching," Charles said. "It makes a funny feeling inside me."

I still hadn't introduced myself to Terry, so I wandered back to the centre where the interviews had wound down and found Terry chatting and shaking hands with well-wishers. I joined the line-up and gave my name, put out my hand and spontaneously kissed him on the cheek. Then I felt as shy as the entire team of the Fournier Mets. He apologized for not greeting me sooner, and I made a mental note of his good manners. We agreed to talk later and I started looking for Doug and Darrell, who were back on the road with the van.

"Oh," they said, as I stuck out my hand again. "We wondered what you looked like." I suspected they'd hoped I was younger.

Later I hopped in the back of the van and for the next thirty-six hours became part of the Marathon of Hope. Terry was already running, nearly out of sight. He was brassily self-confident, because he had started running – in the middle of Saturday afternoon shopping traffic on Hawkesbury's main street – knowing that the Ontario Provincial Police cruiser and the van had to catch up to him. The OPP had generously offered to follow Terry with a cruiser across Ontario. It was protection his family appreciated as much as Terry did: now he could stop looking over his shoulder every few seconds as if afraid a team of Grand Prix drivers were going to swoop him off the road.

Although Doug and Darrell had thoughtfully cleaned the van, presumably for my arrival, there was still the lingering odour of the chemical toilet, which I had at first attributed to the combination of food without refrigeration, sweaty socks, and T-shirts. Doug and Darrell, who had become accustomed to the smell, weren't aware of the effect it had on visitors.

Terry was to run only nine more miles that day. In fact, when he had crossed the Perley Bridge at noon that day, it was not his first entry into Ontario. He had figured that since he didn't have to be at the bridge until noon an entire morning could have been wasted. So they had gotten up at 4:30, when reporters and politicians were still in their beds, and Terry had run ten miles into the province. They had marked the distance, then driven back to Quebec, rested and then run the official first nine miles across the border.

It was peculiar watching him run through the town. Shoppers paused, some almost open-mouthed, their arms full of groceries, as they watched Terry hobble by. We caught up with him on the outskirts of the town just in time to see him disappear into what seemed a large factory with the OPP officer right behind him. Doug deduced it was a washroom stop, and he was right.

The next seven or so miles were open road. Darrell, who was making preparations for Terry's drink break, noticed they were low on ice – ice that was to be used only for Terry's drinking water. The rest of us made do with warm orange and grape pops.

I offered to run into a gas station to ask for ice. The proprietress told me, flatly, no ice. Then she realized I was about to return to the van that said TERRY FOX, MARATHON OF HOPE.

She stopped me and said, "Wait. Is it for Terry?" I told her it was and she said, "Yes, of course, we can give you ice for Terry. We don't have very much, but please take this."

At the next mile marker Terry stopped for a drink. Darrell hurried to have it waiting for him. He also examined the cup to make sure there was no dirt floating with the ice. Terry was fussy. Darrell asked if he wanted gum, cookies, an orange, and wisely had them within easy reach in case Terry became impatient.

They all ignored me. It wasn't rudeness; it was that they each had their duties. I sensed that one simply did not try to chat with Terry on his breaks. I was there to observe, but not interfere.

It was not very comfortable to be around Terry when he was running. Perhaps it was his intensity, the tightness of his concentration; it was almost as though he was protected by a transparent wall. While he was running, no one could penetrate the barrier. Later Terry explained why he wanted everything to be smooth and well organized, even to the point of giving him a clean cup of water: "I wanted things to be as comfortable as they could for me when I wasn't running because I was out there, twenty-six miles a day. The moments that I wasn't running were precious to me and I wanted the other guys to realize that.

"We had a routine, Doug and I, and if something wasn't ready when I came in for my break, we would argue maybe a little bit. There may have been tension, but I didn't feel it the way you did. When you were in the van, I had to pretend you weren't there. Things had to be constant. You know when you've done one mile that the next mile's going to be the same, non-changing, and you can do it again. When things interfere – when something happens on this mile that didn't happen before – it breaks your concentration.

"It was like I had to be alone. It had to be like it was when I was training all by myself at home. I didn't need people around me then. I didn't need the water and I didn't need this or that. I could train by myself at home and I needed the same thing when I was running across Canada. I needed to make the same kind of atmosphere.

"When things changed and new things happened, when new people were around, sometimes it really upset me. When I got in the van and things weren't the same, it made it harder."

I learned quickly to hop out of the van and sit in the roadside grass, to sniff the wild flowers and watch from a distance, whenever Terry took his break.

The Marathon had been offered rooms at the Poplar Motel on Highway 17, a row of low, white-washed bungalows, with metal lawn chairs outside each door. Terry's room was free, the others were given a five-dollar discount. The motel-keeper, a burly, dark-haired man wearing a cook's apron, came out drying his hands, and solemnly reached for Terry's. "Sir," he said, "it's a pleasure to meet you."

Darrell invited me to chat with Terry while he had a snack. I ordered a cup of tea; Terry ordered a cheeseburger, a plate of French fries, a generous slice of apple pie, and a chocolate milkshake. Dinner would come later. We talked about cancer, about how he had never wanted anyone in his family to see him when he was sick. Darrell teased him about the time he'd seen him in the shower without the wig. We talked about running: "People talk about the loneliness of the long-distance runner," Terry said, "but I never feel that. I like to be alone."

In retrospect, I suspect my questioning should have been more thorough. I suppose I was surprised at how ordinary Terry seemed. He had taken on an entire country, but there he was, wolfing down a cheeseburger and goofing around with his kid brother. The tension I had worried about was gone; the intensity that protected him like armour was gone, too, and he was easy and approachable.

He agreed to pose for a few photographs, so we sat in the grass in front of the motel while the camera clicked. *Toronto Star* readers were hot on his trail by this time, and I had a few letters and a gift – a framed copy of his favourite poem – for him.

These were Terry's precious moments of relaxation. But he didn't have them for long. A Cancer Society representative came up to tell him he was expected to speak at a fair in Plantagenet, just down the road. The armour shot up again; muscles in his cheek twitched. You could feel his anger rise.

"Why wasn't I told before?"

Silence.

"I'm not going." His cheek twitched again.

They told him the mayor was waiting for him, they were passing the hat. It wouldn't take long, but he would have to run into the fair.

"It makes me feel so guilty when I say no," he said and agreed to go.

He told Doug to drop him just at the crest of a hill leading to the village, whose main feature was a huge church with a silver spire. Terry stepped wearily out of the van and told Darrell to mark the 200 yards down the hill. He didn't want to have to run them again, in the morning. With a good show of speed, he ran into the village and was welcomed by the mayor, who wore a cowboy hat and called to the crowd in French with a loud hailer.

Terry got quickly to the point: "Any of you could get cancer. I could get it again." Then he signed autographs. Glowing young girls in pink T-shirts, all blond hair and giggles, shyly approached him with their pens and paper; a pensioner, creaky on his feet, wearing a suit jacket and hat despite the heat, dropped a ten-dollar bill in the collection box and gave Terry a robust handshake. Terry showed the same interest in the pensioner as he had in the young girls. He was democratically polite to everyone.

Driving back to the motel, Doug, Darrell, and Terry were silent. It had been a long, hot day and those were their moments for reflection. Darrell, slumped against the car seat, finally said: "I'm thinking about what just happened. What the effect of all that will be, what those little kids who saw Terry will do. It's all for the future."

The green, tidy farmland, lush with summer's crop, rolled by, and the Marathon of Hope drove silently to its home for the night.

Later Darrell called me from my notebook for dinner. Terry ate, it seemed, twice as much as anyone else – a huge steak, a plate of French fries, vegetables, a couple of Cokes. Doug had a plain hamburger. They joked that Doug could live on Terry's leftovers. Terry was animated at the other end of the table, chatting to Cancer Society volunteers. He asked about Quebec and the recent referendum and showed a sparky intelligence and curiosity. He listened well and insisted that Quebec was part of Canada despite its language and cultural differences.

The motel-owners fussed over Terry. They brought him a towering strawberry parfait and pointed out a family sitting nearby who were eating there so they could meet Terry. The family came over to shake his hand. It was easy and comfortable. Then, without a word of farewell, he was gone. It was bedtime and scarcely 7:00 P.M. I watched in surprise as he picked up his bag, walked into his room, and drew the drapes.

It was still five hours before my bedtime, and I was struck with the fear reporters sometimes feel when they realize they may have lost a chance for an interview. I looked at Terry's closed door and wondered if I should knock on it during his quiet time. I walked past the door a few times and decided I would be intruding.

At 4:00 A.M. the next morning I was awake and dressed and sitting outside my room in the steel lawn chair waiting for the others to stir. Doug was the first one out. He knocked on Terry's door. Then the CBC television crew arrrived. They trained their brilliant camera lights on Terry's door – a spotlight in the still, black night. At 4:30 he opened his door slowly and walked into the glare, shielding his eyes for only a moment.

I wasn't sure where to sit in the van – the back where Terry was lying down seemed too close. He told me to sit in the front passenger seat. We drove again in silence. The moon was still high and full. A bank of clouds was reflected in the moonlight and skirted the horizon. Grain silos gleamed in the light. Cattle moved uneasily as we sped by.

Terry lay in the back, wrapped in a soft blue sleeping bag, protected, as in a cocoon, from his duties. He was thinking, he later told me, that he wished it would take an hour to drive to the spot where he was to start running. Darrell was by his side, looking for the pile of rocks by the roadside, which marked the previous day's last mile. Within a few minutes we left him alone on the road and drove ahead exactly one mile.

I stood on the side of the road to wait for him. The sky was still black; there was silence, and the sweet morning smell of good farmland was all around us. The moon cast the only light.

It was Terry's favourite time of day. There were no cars, the temperature was cool, there was no wind. No distractions, no crowds. No speeches. Just Terry doing what he loved doing and did best – running.

He remembered that morning, too: "Some days it was so hard to get going, sometimes it was all pain. I didn't run quickly that morning. I didn't set any speed records, but the miles went so lightly. Right away, that day, they went easily. I just floated. All of a sudden, a mile had gone by."

At dawn Terry was interviewed by a CBC reporter who wired him for sound and then jogged beside him, asking questions as they went. He had told the reporter he didn't think he'd be able to run and answer questions at the same time, but he accepted it as an interesting challenge and loved every minute of it.

Those early miles took thirteen minutes each, compared to his average fourteen-minute miles. By 6:05 A.M. he'd run five miles, and the boys congratulated themselves on their earliest five-mile finish in a long time. In the van, Darrell treated me to a sampler of some Terry's favourite music, including Hank Williams' "Your Cheatin' Heart" and "Jambalaya," while Terry ran. The sun was up, and Terry was beginning to feel its heat. Perspiration had found a familiar resting spot on his chin. At his water break he didn't say a word. He smiled once, just as he set out again, and it was like the sunrise.

Back on the road again, a herd of heifers stopped grazing by the fence and started loping with Terry as he ran past but he didn't notice.

About 8:00 A.M. Terry took his first morning break while Doug prepared breakfast. He made Terry two peanut butter and honey sandwiches on brown bread, gave him a bowl of beans – for energy – a bowl of Cap'n Crunch cereal, and a couple of Cokes.

The rest of us would find a restaurant later. I chatted with Terry as he ate and once again he was that amiable, patient young fellow from the night before. It was difficult to find even a trace of the intensity I had found so intimidating. Those psychological walls he build around himself to give him a runner's tunnel vision were knocked down.

He explained why he didn't like to have two-legged runners too close to him as he ran. "I'm running on one leg. It may not look like I'm running fast, but I'm going as hard as I can. It bothers me, people coming up beside me. I want to make those guys work. I can't stand making it easy for them. I'm really competitive. When they run with me, they're usually running for only two or three miles; for me it might be my twenty-sixth mile.

"Some people can't figure out what I'm doing. It's not a walk-hop, it's not a trot; it's running, or as close as I can get to running, and it's harder than doing it on two legs. It makes me mad when people call this a walk. If I was walking it wouldn't be anything. It's the difference between walking up a hill and walking up a mountain." The message was, of course, that Terry was on the mountain, not the hill.

Then the conversation turned to a topic dear to Terry's heart – accomplishment. He said he spent a lot of his time thinking, about life, about man's carelessness on this planet. "Man is supposed to be an intelligent species, yet we keep polluting. We seem to want to wipe ourselves right off the earth, and no one is doing anything about it. That bothers me, everyone seems to have given up hope of trying. I haven't. It isn't easy and it isn't supposed to be, but I'm accomplishing something. How many people give up a lot to do something good? I'm sure we would have found a cure for cancer twenty years ago if we had really tried.

"It bothers me, too, that so many kids are brought up the way they are. Why do we have crime? Why do we have so many thinking about themselves? You might think I'm a dreamer, but how many people would have said I could run across Canada? I know that there is $10 million out there to be given – if only everyone would try." Wondering if Terry ever explored his subconscious, I asked if he remembered any of his night dreams. He immediately said he didn't. It was apparent he set store in the real world, the tangible, not the unexplored backwaters of his mind.

Then it was rest time. Terry and Doug disappeared with the van over a low hill to find a quiet, cool place to sleep for a few hours.

While they rested, Jack Hilliard, the Cancer Society district representative who was responsible for Terry in eastern Ontario (and who also drove his car with the newly acquired and portable sign which said SLOW, RUNNER AHEAD on one side and DONATIONS ACCEPTED HERE on the other), met with Jack Lambert, the district director who would take over in the Peterborough area. We drove through Rockland, while Darrell showed his prankish side and woke the sleepy town by calling on the hailer: "Good morning, Rockland."

Already I found the routine tedious, and yet I had been with them less than twenty-four hours. Darrell claimed he was never bored. "There wasn't a time when I said, 'What am I doing here?' because every day was different. You knew you'd meet someone new. Everyday you were getting closer to home. I never wanted to go home, yet I dreamed of that day when he ran his last mile. You'd think I would be bored, getting up at four every day and sitting in that van, for how many hours. But it seemed that time went by fast. I never even got tired of getting his stuff ready or of making his sandwiches or giving him all that junk food."

By mid-afternon, Terry was pushing himself hard along the main street of Rockland, quiet on this Sunday afternoon in midsummer. Terry's OPP escort turned on his siren, and the streets were filled. People poured out of their homes in their summer cottons. Those who were fit ran behind Terry. The kids on their bikes circled him like bees around the sweetest flower. Women ran up to Doug and asked if he would take their donations of two dollars. Those by the side of the road covered their mouths, ovals of surprise. They focused hard on the runner. Then they clapped. They shouted after him. Some ran back into their homes to get their children or their parents.

It was like a parade. I watched from the backseat and talked to Doug. He had seen a lot of Canada from that viewpoint: "We eat, we go to bed and we pass through these towns and we don't get to see nothin'!"

With all the activity swirling around us, Doug turned to me and told me about Terry's heart condition. It was a deep secret, he said. Terry never talked about it. Despite the claustrophobia and heat in the van, I felt a chill, understanding there was more at stake than I had dreamed. Perhaps Doug had wanted to make sure that I understood how much Terry was sacrificing. Perhaps he wanted to make sure I knew that no matter how loudly Terry was cheered, all the hoop-la was incidental to his commitment.

Then Darrell rushed up, sparkling with excitement, and broke the tension: "All right, all *right!*" he said as he watched the town applaud Terry. It was clear why he was on this journey, why he was never bored, why he never grew tired of his duties. He was in centre ring, serving his brother on the biggest wing-ding adventure he would ever know. He was watching Terry being embraced by a nation.

Before the opening kick at a Canadian Football League exhibition game in Ottawa, Terry had to decide which leg to kick with.

Until he acquired his police escort in Ontario, Terry was extremely vulnerable on the highways. Occasionally, drivers even tried to force him off the road.

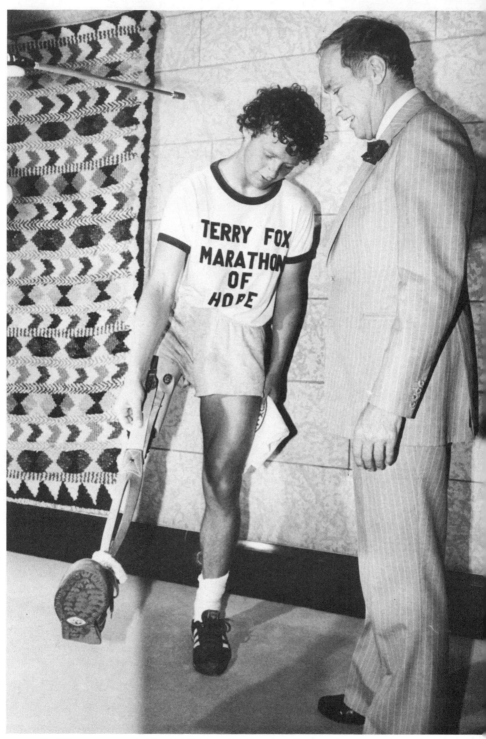

At his meeting with Prime Minister Trudeau in Ottawa, Terry demonstrated how his prosthesis worked.

In Ottawa, Terry ran past the Parliament Buildings.

CP PHOTO

Ontario greeted Terry with wreaths and kisses.

Doug Alward addressed a crowd at a fund-raising rally in Mississauga. An old schoolfriend of Terry's, Doug accompanied Terry on the Marathon, driving the van and helping where he could.

Toronto gave Terry the largest reception he had received thus far. His entry
into Nathan Phillips Square at City Hall attracted thousands.

Terry's pride as he stood with his father in Nathan Phillips Square was evident. Darryl Sittler, who ran with him down University Avenue in Toronto, gave Terry his sweater.

In the Scarborough Civic Centre, Terry shook hands with Bonnie O'Neill. Standing next to him was Anne Marie Von Zuben, who had had kidney cancer since age three and whose courage inspired Terry long after the meeting.

# Chapter Eight

If Darrell felt out of place wearing his shorts and T-shirt into Government House to meet Governor General Ed Schreyer and his wife, Lily, Terry certainly didn't. He was brought a glass of orange juice on a silver tray, which he gulped down just as Schreyer came forward to meet him. Darrell remembered feeling stupid and uncomfortable as he accidently dumped a glass of orange juice in the driveway of that grand old house. Besides, there were, Darrell remembered, "all those guys from Reach for the Top wearing suits."

For Terry the fun was just beginning. It would last at least a month as he purposely ran 700 miles out of his way through densely populated southern Ontario and the key fund-raising cities of Toronto, Hamilton, and London. Doug was left to shake his head in amazement. "Ontario was like eternity. We felt that we weren't going anywhere. Terry had conquered five provinces in two and a half months, and Ontario was equal to all of those. Two things I remember about Ontario: people everywhere, and money."

Ontario was also the start of the warm and tireless grass-roots support for Terry that would eventually vitalize the entire country. The children from the grade five class in Odessa Public School (a village of 400, 165 miles east of Toronto) raised fifteen dollars by saving the pennies and nickels left over from their milk money. Their teacher, Brian Norris, promised to match whatever the children finally raised.

On a larger scale, but with equal feeling, two friends, Garth Walker of Mississauga, Ontario, and Jim Brown of Kingston, decided they'd like to give Terry a gift from the province. They

115

started their own fund-raising campaign and asked for sponsors on their 300-mile overnight dash from Toronto to Ottawa by bicycle. They raised more than $50,000 and cycled in the dark through thunderstorms to present the cash and pledges to Terry in person. But before he would meet Garth and Jim, Terry ran to one of the warmest welcomes of the run, and until that time the largest reception ever:

"When I ran through that tiny little Sparks Street Mall, the road was so narrow, yet people were running behind me and all these other people were lined up, clapping for me. It was quite a long way down the road where all the people were and I was just sprinting. I was floating through the air and I didn't even feel a thing. I felt so great. That type of memory you can never take away."

Even bigger times lay ahead, but business came first; Terry had to finish five more miles that day.

The next day, having debated whether it was wiser to use his left leg or his artificial one, Terry kicked the opening ball of a Canadian Football League exhibition game between Ottawa and Saskatchewan – with his good leg. He received a standing ovation from more than 16,000 fans at Lansdowne Park, and for the once quiet boy who was now very confident, it was more exciting than watching Darryl Sittler score an overtime goal. He was stunned by the crowd's response. Realizing that all kinds of ordinary Canadians were deeply affected by his dream made the effort seem all the more worthwhile.

He ran twenty miles that day and finished in time to drive back to Ottawa to meet Prime Minister Pierre Trudeau on Parliament Hill. Trudeau was just back from Venice and hadn't heard of the runner who was stirring up the country. What could have been the highlight of Terry's trip became a disappointment.

They were scheduled to meet in Trudeau's Centre Block office, but as the Prime Minister walked up the stairs from the House of Commons, he was surprised to find Terry, his crew, and a gang of reporters waiting for him in the hallway. So they had the meeting there, against a background of stone walls and camera lights.

They were a study in contrasts: Terry's curls were damp with perspiration and clung to his forehead. He wore a T-shirt that said CANCER UNIT, GRAND FALLS, NEWFOUNDLAND, his regulation grey, sweat-spotted shorts and a dusty grey sock (which he hadn't changed since the start of the run) on his artificial leg. He was eager for Trudeau to run a token half mile with him, believing it would have "a big effect on the campaign." Trudeau, whose mind may have still been on the grilling he'd received from the Opposition during Question Period, was as aloof as Terry was animated. His striped summer suit was as crisp as the fresh flower on his lapel.

Since there had been no time for a briefing by his press aides, Trudeau asked Terry basic questions: Which way was he running? Then he watched as Terry demonstrated how his artificial leg worked. Camera lights flashed down the stately hallway and the meeting was over. Darrell observed: "It was as if Trudeau was talking to Terry and thinking about something else."

Terry told his diary it was an honour to meet *Mr. Trudeau who is a nice man. Unfortunately, he's very busy and can't run with me.*

Later Terry told me: "The meeting wasn't what I'd hoped for. He didn't seem to know much about the run. I'm not blaming him – it was great meeting him – I just thought he knew more about it. He didn't even know I was running for cancer."

Two days later, on July 6, the *Sunday Star* urged Trudeau to show the admiration of our nation and give Terry's run a boost: "This is a Prime Minister who has twirled a yo-yo on a state visit, pirouetted behind the Queen, slid down banisters, publicly somersaulted into swimming pools and canoed some of Canada's wildest rivers. For a man of such prowess, a half-mile run would scarcely make a dent in the prime ministerial schedule – and the cause is certainly deserving."

As he ran into Ontario's heartland, Terry could barely express the effect he had on people. People were going wild for him. His diary entries merely said: *unreal reception . . . tremendous support here . . . these people are really trying . . . best so far*, and on and on. He had been fitted for two new $2,000 legs, which would be made by a Hull prosthetist and one of Canada's most skilful craftsmen, Armand Viau. The cost was borne by the War Amputations Association. While he was being received more warmly than ever before, he was also running in considerable discomfort from the large cysts on his stump. He was also having difficulty sleeping, partly because of the heat, partly because of poorly soundproofed hotel rooms and his own inner tension.

People were now lining the highway to wait for him. They'd

wait in the rain, and hail down Doug's van to make a pledge. Sometimes they'd explain that they had a sister who had also lost a leg to cancer. Sometimes they'd say nothing, but would just applaud on the highway as Terry ran by.

The drivers of Voyageur buses were starting to stop regularly whenever they saw him. The driver would simply make an announcement on the loudspeaker, then walk to the back of the bus taking donations from passengers.

Once, near Millwood, Ontario, Terry collapsed in the van from exhaustion – his face brilliant, his breath laboured, his eyes closed as if blocking out the light and the pain – with a wrinkled $100 bill, still damp from perspiration, clasped tightly in his hand. He was oblivious to everything – visitors, well wishers, even the money. He needed a rest. Jack Lambert, a Cancer Society district director, had made arrangements for Terry to take his break at the home of Olga Fallis, a Cancer Society volunteer. When Terry lumbered wearily into the cool of her ninety-seven-year-old classic brick farmhouse, he was asked how long he'd like to sleep.

He smiled wanly and said, "Till I wake up!"

Doug followed behind him, bringing fresh clothes and a can of spaghetti to be warmed for Terry's lunch.

In the next few days, Doug noticed a change. Terry wasn't greeted merely as the one-legged runner: he was greeted in the more glittering light of a celebrity, a folk hero, a Canadian wonder. He was filmed by NBC's "Real People" and ran with hostess-interviewer Sarah Purcell. Their picture together appeared on the front page of the Toronto *Sun* in brassy colour.

That night Terry walked into an Oshawa shopping mall and Doug recalled: "It was as if he was a rock star. People were crowding around wanting to touch him. It was packed from one end to the other, and I couldn't even see him when he started to leave. Women and girls, the teenage generation, were starting to chase him. I'm sure he started to wonder, 'What's happening?' "

The next morning, the *Toronto Star* arranged to have Rolly, Betty, and Judith delivered by a long, blue limosine to a quiet street corner in Whitby, just before dawn, for a surprise reunion with Terry as he came over a hill. The air was fine, and women stood on the sidewalk, wearing sweaters over their nighties, waiting for Terry to run into sight. The family embraced in front of the cameras. Then Terry, ever of independent mind, refused to pose any more and rested for a few minutes in a doughnut shop. While Terry attacked his beans, his parents surveyed him and approved of what they saw. He looked healthier and stronger than he had when they left him in Nova Scotia. They ached to be alone with Terry – as Rolly said, "It's hard to talk to your son in public" – but Terry, in those days, could have had anything he wanted except privacy.

As Betty and Rolly watched Terry carefully, he chatted amiably about how nice it was to see his parents, adding he felt they were always with him anyway. Then a voice on the radio in the back of the doughnut shop told listeners about Terry Fox and how everyone could see him on Highway 2 later that day. Terry refused to get in the limosine; he said it was pretentious.

Since Terry's schedule was unpredictable, people were willing to wait hours for his arrival and be content to give him a shout when he finally passed by. John and Edna Neale, a retired Pickering couple, waited two hours under a steamy sky. As Terry ran by them they said he was just what was needed to give us a little pride in our own people, the same kind of pride Americans have in abundance.

A pair of thirteen-year-old girls, Linda Rowe and Patricia Morrison, were anxious to get Terry's autograph. But those days were over, too; he simply didn't have time, Doug explained, as he returned the girls' crumpled scraps of paper. "We want to remember him when we get older," Linda said.

On the outskirts of metropolitan Toronto, Molly and Fred Danniels sat in civilized splendour in garden chairs out on their front lawn. They sipped coffee, ate cheesecake, and waited most of the day for Terry. Molly had racked her brain, wanting to do something, anything, for Terry, so she painted a sign at least four feet square that said simply GOOD LUCK, TERRY. Terry didn't run by their house that day, so they were up again at 5:00 A.M. to catch him the next morning.

His impact was close to universal. Take the cab driver who hauled his kids out of bed at 4:30 and drove to Kingston Road in Scarborough so they would see Terry and never forget. He passed twenty-five dollars to Doug and said, "It's from me and the kids." Or the pre-dawn motorcyclist, all black leather and malevolence shrouded in his helmet, who pulled up beside Doug, thrust a twenty-dollar bill through the open window, and drove away wordlessly.

In Scarborough, Terry made what many believed to be his best and certainly his most moving speech. It seemed to be his habit to discuss publicly what was bothering him privately. Just as he had once confessed he was sometimes hard on Doug, he now stood beneath a swirl of curved balconies, laden by this time with adoring fans, in the great airy cavern of the Scarborough Civic Centre, and told several thousand people that his fame was not meant to be part of the run. He wasn't interested in wealth or notoriety; he was just a guy running across the country to collect money for cancer research. Don't forget, he told them, and focus your thoughts on the Marathon of Hope, not on me. Then he said, somewhat alarmingly, that the Marathon had to continue even without him. Doug shook his head in amazement as he listened to Terry: "I can't believe the kind of person he's become since grade eight."

Terry was tearful, his voice husky and strained, as he spoke. In his hand he twirled a bright yellow daffodil, the gift of Anne Marie Von Zuben, a victim of kidney cancer since age three, who looked much younger than her thirteen years. The sight of Anne Marie, whose mother called her a miracle baby because of her many recoveries, whose hopeful smile and positive attitude seemed the essence of the Marathon of Hope, was almost too much for Terry. For a man who was noted for his emotional restraint, who was at times an interviewer's nightmare because it seemed he was saying the same things over and over again without giving any real insight into his character, this was a rare moment of revelation. It didn't come after hours of intense questioning; it came in front of a crowd of ordinary people, spontaneously, from his heart. The moment was almost too difficult to bear because what he said made one ache with understanding of his ordeal and comprehend better what made Terry run.

He remembered that moment, too: "Everyone sounded close and warm. Just looking at people, way up on the top row, curled all the way around, cheering and clapping, I felt really close to them, warm and emotional, and I think they felt the same way, too. The biggest thing was when the little girl brought up the flower. She's the one who really broke me down. The way the room was built, I could really feel the vibrations coming back to me. It wasn't planned. It's just the way I felt at the time. That moment, right then, was one of the highest."

As if emotion on that scale wasn't enough for one day, Terry was expected to repeat the performance at Nathan Phillips Square in front of Toronto's City Hall. The prelude was a surprise meeting with his brother Fred, also flown in courtesy of the *Toronto Star*, and the long-awaited introduction to former Maple Leaf hockey team captain, Darryl Sittler.

It was a bright, hot summer day, and the temperature reached 30°C. With Doug, Darrell, Fred, Judith, and Darryl Sittler flanking him, Terry ran down Toronto's University Avenue amid the jumble of lunch-hour traffic. The street, a wide, divided thoroughfare, is dotted with well-known Toronto landmarks including the prestigious Toronto General Hospital, the Hospital for Sick Children, and Mount Sinai Hospital, and Queen's Park, the Ontario legislative buildings.

More spectacular was the response of the people. Women in hair curlers peered out of chic Yorkville beauty salons and called their stylists over to have a look as Terry ran by. Beautiful women lost their dignity, hiked up their summer skirts and ran on high heels as if they were kids to get a second look at him. Medical technicians, their white lab coats flapping, ran down the street beside him, and a hardy corps of volunteers wove in and out of traffic to fill garbage bags with donations.

In photographs of the two of them running, Sittler is seen smiling easily beside Terry, whose face is contorted into that familiar grimace. It was clear there was a great difference between running on two good legs and running on one made of fibreglass and steel.

The group burst into the square, which police estimated held about 10,000, and made its way to a platform loaded with politicians, company executives, entertainers, and Cancer Society officers, led by actor Al Waxman, the society's honorary chairman. Sittler gave Terry his 1980 NHL all-star team sweater, number 27 and called Terry a superstar: "I've been around athletes a long time and I've never seen any with his courage and stamina."

Betty, Rolly, Fred, and Judith were led on stage, and as Rolly approached Terry, he spontaneously lifted his son's hand in victory. Terry quickly and modestly drew his hand back down. Then Waxman introduced Terry as the "toast of Toronto and the hero of all Canada."

Terry faced the crowd, on whose faces tears mingled with beads of perspiration, and told them a little of the problems of heroism. "It almost hurts me to walk down a road and have people grab my hand and ask for my autograph and not sit and talk. It hurt me . . . when I'm finished I'm not going to be on the front page, but I'm going to be just as happy without the publicity. . . .

"Those claps, take them for yourself. If you've given a dollar, you are part of the Marathon of Hope. That ovation was for you, wherever you are in Canada."

The Cancer Society estimated about $100,000 – including $59,000 in pledges from CKFM radio, which reported listeners were phoning in pledges at a rate of $4,000 per hour – was gathered in one day. That night Terry threw the opening pitch of a Toronto Blue Jays baseball game and received a standing ovation at Exhibition Park.

The next morning, he flew to Niagara Falls and was handed a cheque for $100 by the mayor, Wayne Thompson, and was greeted by fifty people. It was an embarrassment to the city, fumed Cliff Gregory, president of the Cancer Society, because the town offered Terry neither moral nor monetary support. Terry was also reluctant to visit a Niagara Falls marineland show when he was told he wouldn't be able to solicit funds. Nothing could make him more furious than the thought that he was being used commercially. He'd go out of his way to speak to people, but the basis for all visits had to be the possibility of raising money.

Later that day, Terry was back in Toronto, and I caught him for a few minutes before he started his afternoon run along Danforth Avenue, the city's traffic-choked Greek strip. We had a hasty interview:

"What do you think of the attention?"

"It's great that they like me, but they should give a buck, too," he said.

A few more questions and I said, "Thanks, Terry. Good luck on your walk."

I felt like a clod as his eyes turned steely blue and he said: "I'm running."

It was a muggy, slightly overcast, but very hot day. Volunteers were recruited off the street to collect donations from drivers

122

stalled behind Terry and the Metro motorcycle police who preceded him. One dark-haired young man ordered his girlfriend to take over the wheel of his red Corvette, while he ran eight miles into town helping to collect money. He refused to give his name. A photographer turned his back on a wedding party to photograph Terry.

"Top fellow," called a crisp British voice from a passing car.

"Magnificent, man," yelled another admirer. The loudest roars of approval came from crowds who stood outside bars to watch Terry pass.

Later Terry's family and a couple of Cancer Society volunteers emptied the garbage bags filled with money onto the creamy carpet at the Four Seasons Hotel. Betty hadn't watched Terry run; she found it too painful. Terry sat back beaming with a bottle of beer. They counted $5,326.26 – collected in about two hours of running. Included in one of those bags was a letter from a Toronto woman who wrote that Terry had helped her stop feeling sorry for herself. She vowed to lose weight and she pledged Terry one dollar for every pound lost. Her husband, she added, would match her dollar for dollar. The last line read: "P.S. This could mean $200."

When the last pile of pennies was tucked away in a drawer, Doug puffed in, looking more confused than usual. "Where'd everyone go?" he asked. In his enthusiasm, he had run along Bloor Street for an extra mile, long after Terry had turned in at the hotel. Doug probably would have kept running, savouring the exercise and his joyful release from the driver's seat, if a puzzled Metro police constable hadn't politely asked him where he was going and pointed him back to the hotel.

That night the family relaxed together and dined in the world's highest restaurant, which is just below the world's highest disco, atop the CN Tower. The lights on the tower's top, which usually read SPARKLES, said TERRY FOX that night. Terry started to doze over his half-finished meal, but he came alive later in the tower's basement penny arcade.

It was a rare evening. For once he had a chance to unwind. All the Fox offspring jumped into bumper cars and rammed one another hard, and laughed even harder. Then Terry's leg was jogged loose, and he had to limp, holding his artificial limb, which was hidden under corduroy pants, off the platform. Suddenly he was surrounded by admirers and autograph-seekers.

"Nobody recognized me until my leg fell off," he laughed.

On his route through southern Ontario – to Oakville, Hamilton, Brantford, London, Kitchener, Guelph, and Brampton – Terry was fêted unrelentingly. The strength of the response to his fundrasing drive was totally unexpected. For example, Joan Gibb, an Oakville Cancer Society volunteer, reported that a week before Terry arrived about $235 had been collected. She decided to have an oversized cheque made up for the presentation. But when Darrell arrived for advance drum-beating around 4:00 P.M. she had to alter the total to $8,600, and when Terry turned up two hours later, the figure had jumped to $11,239. Incredibly, they had raised another $3,000 in a mere two hours.

Crowds were as constant and in some ways as debilitating as the high temperatures. Everyone wanted a piece of Terry. They wanted him to make speeches, to accept cheques, and to do so in person, for in the case of Terry Fox there could be no substitutions.

In Hamilton, it was reported, Terry was mobbed by teenagers and women after he spoke at the Royal Botanical Gardens and raised $4,500. A story sent across the wire service described Terry, possibly for the first time, as being "irritable" and needing a nap. It was also in Hamilton, however, that 1960 Canadian Marathon champion Gord Dickson gave Terry his gold medal, saying the young fellow was running the greatest race of all.

While he would never accept money for himself (although it was common for someone to press fifty dollars into his hand and say, "Keep it. This is for you. For yourself.") Terry gratefully accepted mementos. All cash gifts went to the Cancer Society.

In mid-July, a curious item appeared in the Guelph *Daily Mercury*. A seventeen-year-old high-school student, Marlene Lott, was quoted as saying there was "nothing extra-curricular" about her relationship with Terry, despite a Toronto *Sun* photograph showing her kneeling in the van, wiping Terry's neck with a towel. She said she had developed a "slight friendship" with Terry's sister, Judy, during her five-day stay in Toronto.

Marlene and Terry did go out for dinner a few times, but although they may have briefly contemplated a romance, the demands of the run took precedence over affairs of the heart.

The fact remained, however, that Terry was an attractive young man who sometimes did get very lonely, although he was always the centre of a mob of people. Young women were intensely attracted to him, and once in a while, one might join the Marathon of Hope for a day or two along the road, but Terry said he never fell in love.

Terry realized that he had to be above reproach. He had become a personality whose every move was subject to public scrutiny. Once the *Star* reported that he had gone on a date, a fact he felt was too personal for public knowledge. Rather than subject himself, or anyone else, to the media's probing eye, he simply said to himself, no girls.

"You know I hardly ever had the chance to meet anybody. I was just too busy, and when I did, it was publicized. But my goal was so strong overall that it didn't really bother me. It didn't really affect me, but there were some times when I wished that I could meet somebody, or I'd see a girl and be attracted back and want to ask her out. I guess that just makes me more human. But it never was a big sacrifice. I knew my goal. I could wait."

Occasionally Terry needed someone to talk to about matters that were troubling him. He called me at home one Saturday afternoon. First, he said he was sorry he hadn't been able to talk to me for the previous Running-with-Terry report. Then, warming to his subject, he complained that he couldn't make a move without someone (me) reporting on it. Lastly – and I suspect most importantly – he asked how I thought the public would react if a girl joined the Marathon of Hope for a couple of weeks. "You know me," Terry said, "I have high morals." While I knew Terry's principles were irreproachable, after some discussion we both agreed that deep in the heart of church-going conservative, southern Ontario an unchaperoned female aide wouldn't do Terry's cause any good. He didn't really need convincing; I suspect he knew it all along. He just needed to talk about being lonely for a few minutes, and that was that.

The days were difficult for Terry. Temperatures soared to 38°C, and a muggy wind slowed his progress, yet he continued to put in twenty-six miles a day, or very close to it. In London he was escorted by a hundred runners who had each raised fifty dollars in pledges. They called themselves the $5,000 Club, but might as well have been called the $11,000 Club – because that's how much they raised. Terry also ran with seventeen-year-old Tony Coutinho, a leukemia survivor for twelve and a half years and the subject of the Emmy-award-winning documentary *Fighting Back*.

In Stratford, Terry got a kiss from British actress and festival star Maggie Smith between fittings for a new leg by his British Columbia prosthetist, Ben Speicher, who had been flown to London courtesy of the War Amputations of Canada. Other prosthetists who had seen Terry's stump observed that it was in remarkably good condition considering he had run 2,256 miles on it.

Terry was elated to see Ben. "I started out on a leg he built and I'm back using it again. I had two new legs made in Quebec, but they haven't stood up. I'll feel a lot better when I have the spare leg made. I've been worried about the leg breaking down and losing a lot of time waiting," he told reporters.

As he ran through the bland southern Ontario heat – heat that clung to him and sapped his strength, that made the air dense, as though he were running in slow motion – Terry heard radio reports that he was sick and in bad shape.

"Don't believe everything you hear," he warned a Vancouver interviewer. "One of the radio stations out here said I would be in the hospital for three days. No way."

The Marathon had its funny moments, too. Darrell often sat on the hood of a donations car, as it crawled along the highway, accepting money from drivers as they passed. Once a driver pulled up to Darrell, apparently not understanding what was going on. He looked in the hat, saw all the money, and took out five dollars. Darrell looked at him in amazement and said, "Thank you," as the driver pulled away and disappeared down the road.

Some of the fund-raising gimmicks brought a few chuckles as well. Freddie Sless of Hamilton raised $912 for Terry by sitting in a huge vat of banana-lemon custard. "I didn't notice the smell at first," he told reporters, "but then I was starting to get hazy." Brad Barber of Mississauga put on a pair of knee pads and vowed to break a world record for crawling, in Terry's honour. He made it eleven and a half miles, still short of the fourteen-mile record, before giving up. He raised $5,000.

The Marathon machine was in high gear by this time. Terry Fox was a celebrity, and the finest proof of his fame were the dollars that rolled relentlessly into the Cancer Society coffers. They poured in so quickly the society was at a loss to count them efficiently. It simply had not expected such a generous outpouring of money. By July 21, the society reported that $750,000 in cash had been counted, but they couldn't estimate the pledges. Ron

Calhoun guessed that $20,000 had been collected on the road in one day in southern Ontario.

Terry appeared worn out occasionally, but his regenerative powers were formidable. One night's good sleep could cure a week of stress, but frequently he was not being allowed even that. Once Terry told a reporter: "People want me everywhere. The Cancer Society people have been really great, but they don't understand that I get tired at night." Once organizers even expected him to be in two places at the same time. Forgetting that Terry had promised, months before, to attend a lunch in Toronto with 140 senior executives, the Cancer Society scheduled him to speak in Brampton at the same time. It was awkward. Some believed that Terry preferred to spend an afternoon with Canada's corporate elite, instead of the common working folk of Brampton. The Brampton *Daily Times* even accused the Cancer Society of using Terry to further its fund-raising ambitions.

If only the good people of Brampton could have seen how unimpressed Terry was by the hotel silver-plate, the chilled strawberries, the fresh-cut flowers, and the sight of some of Canada's leading business lights shaking his hand, patting his back. There were 140 of them, magnificent in their finely tailored three-piece suits, and there was Terry, in his familiar T-shirt and shorts, calm, confident and apparently interested in everyone he met.

The then mayor of Toronto came over to Terry saying, "I'm John Sewell. I'm the mayor." Pauline McGibbon, the province's lieutenant-governor at the time, was there chatting with Terry, her husband, Don, by her side. The party was thrown by Isadore Sharp, who presented Terry with a cheque for $10,600 – two dollars every mile Terry would run across Canada. The idea was that the 139 guests would respond with similar donations. The original notion of corporate sponsorships came from Eddie Creed, a Four Seasons director, who realized "somebody had to get behind Terry and create some excitement and recognize what he was doing. The Marathon of Hope needed a corporation behind it. We are across Canada . . . but little did we realize what a fantastic guy this kid is," he said.

Terry believed his speech to the executives was one of his best and confided to his diary that he felt he made a good impression. In fact, he charmed them inside out. He told them about cancer research and about the drug that had improved his odds for survival from 15 per cent to between 50 and 70 per cent. He told them it was more difficult losing his hair than losing his leg, but "that turned out good because I never had curly hair before and now I do." They heard his delightful chuckle as he laughed at his own vanity, and they watched his face tense as he described his young friend from the cancer clinic who kept him awake with his screams of pain.

He showed, in fact, how artful a public speaker he had become. He told them that, although it sounded crass, money, their money, was needed to fight cancer. Then he told them how other Canadians were responding – a man had given Terry his $500 guitar with tears in his eyes. Young kids had given him ten cents – everything they had. Old pensioners and welfare recipients were giving more than they could probably afford. "It's important to give what you can, to give money, because you want to find a cure. It feels good to give."

He told them people could get cancer and die from it and still be winners. He told them he would never be called a quitter. Then he repeated a couple of sentences that made a few in his audience feel uneasy. Not that it was prophetic, not that Terry had second sight or even a premonition of what was to come; it was just that he seemed so healthy, he beamed and sparkled with strength and good humour. "If I stop," he said, "it's because something's happened. I'm in bed but I'm still going to think of myself as a winner."

He knew just how good it felt to give.

Later, Terry knocked knees with Bobby Orr – the former hockey star and the Canadian Terry had most wanted to meet – who presented him with a cheque for $25,000 from his sponsors, Planter's Peanuts. It was, Terry told his diary, the highlight of his trip.

The next days arched in highs and lows for Terry. He wanted to run, only run. Yet he found himself driving the van thirty miles at night to receptions, and that drained him. He found that Bill Vigars and Jack Lambert had arranged for him to run an extra ten miles out of his way to Barrie, along Highway 11, instead of Highway 27. He was infuriated and yet felt powerless. Bill had agreed on the longer route without consulting Terry, believing Terry would be pleased with the extra fund-raising. Terry insisted

128

he would take the shorter route and Bill begged him to reconsider. Otherwise, he said, as they sat side by side in a motel room, the Cancer Society volunteers who had been working in that area might quit. Bill might even lose his job.

Terry, silent with rage, hurt because he no longer had control over his own run, and close to exhaustion, ran the extra ten miles up Highway 11. He didn't speak to Bill for three days.

The two had become close friends by this time. Bill, struggling with a marital separation, was on the road every day with Terry for two and a half months, often with his children. Sometimes Terry played with the children at night, because they were a delightful distraction from the rigours of his day. He could relax with little children.

"Bill let other Cancer Society people know that only one thing was supposed to be planned for me at night and he'd tell them what time I'd arrive. If I didn't make it to a town I would drive to it. He was there for all those special things. But he was more than that because he became a close friend. I think he was a real good guy, friendly, joking all the time. I could relax with him. He was somebody who began to care a lot about me. I could talk to him about anything I wanted and ask advice. Before he came, I really didn't have anything like that. There are things that I can talk to Doug about, and he's great, but there are some things I can't – I don't know why. And Darrell, well, he was my younger brother.

"If something was bugging me, if there was a girl or somebody who wanted to get involved with the trip and I didn't know how to say she or he couldn't, Bill would do it for me. He would do the dirty work. At the same time, sometimes things got boggled up because he wasn't quite sure. He made some mistakes, too, but I don't hold anything against him. Just as I got upset at Darrell and Doug, sometimes I got upset with Bill. He's not the type of person who could take it, and sometimes he would leave for a few days just because of that and then come back. On our way to Sault Ste. Marie, he left for three days. I was upset because Doug and Darrell never left. They were always there. Bill was supposed to be travelling with us all the way but he needed a rest inside to keep going. It bothered me. I thought it was a weakness that the rest of us didn't have."

Bill saw himself as mother and father to the whole crew. He was sometimes caught in the middle and felt his patience was ebbing. Near Barrie he thought Terry was getting a little cocky and he was annoyed when he heard exchanges such as this:

Passerby (looking at the miles marked on the van, which showed Terry was 200 miles shy of halfway): "Congratulations on being halfway."

Terry: "Can't you add?"

Terry, however, doesn't remember the incident. Perhaps the demands were too much for him. Perhaps that's the only way Terry could react. Whenever he took a break somebody wanted his autograph, somebody wanted to talk to him, or touch him. On the road there were no buffers; he was exposed and open.

In the evenings when the receptions were over and the miles were tucked away for the night, Terry had a different personality. He was light, not intense and demanding; he was the jokester everyone remembered. The undercurrent those days may have been tension, but the bottom line, the sea bed that supported them all, was love and deep respect. Doug, Darrell, and Bill were understanding and forgiving; often they knew that Terry was right: they were bungling at his expense.

Darrell remembered once trying to alter the mileage indicator that reported how far Terry had run and had yet to run. Darrell changed the miles but he had the numbers wrong. Terry yelled at him to get it right. Darrell changed it again. But he was wrong a second time. Terry took him aside and patiently explained all Darrell had to do was add four.

"And I was trying so hard to get it right!" Darrell said.

As they approached Gravenhurst and Terry's twenty-second birthday, the Marathon plotted how they could surprise him. Darrell was assigned to walk towards Terry with a cake and a naughty smile and decorate Terry with the whipped cream. But Darrell lost his nerve, perhaps believing that Terry's humour might not be up to scratch. He decided it would be safer to deliver the cake into Terry's hand. Terry ran twelve miles through the rain, past crowds of people who burst into "Happy Birthday" at every corner. It was comical and touching. Some bystanders covered themselves in plastic garbage bags as they waited until he ran by; others protected their heads with paper bags.

As Terry walked into the Holiday Inn, Darrell made his respectful approach, cake in hand. Terry received it gently, then hurled it towards Darrell, towards Scott Hamilton who was recording the fun on film, and towards Bill. They were all laughing, covered in cake, as they trotted into the Holiday Inn for breakfast – Black Forest cake and Coke. Terry's sole birthday wish had been to run twenty-six miles; he simply wouldn't hear talk of taking a day, or even half a day, off. Because of all the festivities, he only had time for twenty miles that day – but what a day!

He was invited for dinner at the Beaver Creek Correctional Camp, a minimum-security federal penitentiary where the inmates had raised $900 in a car wash and a barbeque for his Marathon. One of the men, a long-time offender, stood spontaneously to tell Terry: "I've been through some of the toughest jails in Canada and been with some of the hardest men, but you have more guts and courage than any I ever met."

Compliments also came from the other side of the law. Ontario Provincial Police constable John Lennox of the Bala detachment was Terry's escort through cottage country. He called his assignment the proudest days of his life. "If all kids had his honesty, guts, and desire, I'd be out of a job."

The fun was just beginning. Terry was rushed back to the Gravenhurst Civic Centre where 2,000 people gathered to sing "Happy Birthday." Terry's gifts included his new limb from Ben Speicher, a toilet seat inscribed "To a good shit" (a reference, no doubt, to Terry's bowel habits and the van's toilet), and a *Playboy* magazine. The latter two were Bill's ideas. Telegrams poured in from across Canada, including a long one from the British Columbia Cancer Society, which bore 1,000 signatures and a donation of $4,000.

The biggest thrill of all – the sort that made Terry's face positively radiate excitement – was the news that Gravenhurst, a town of 8,000, raised $14,000. It was close to double Terry's dream of one dollar from every Canadian. Everyone shared a seventy-pound cake decorated with a map of Canada that showed Terry's route in red and green icing, and marked Gravenhurst with a red cherry. It was donated by Peter Rebelein of the Gravenhurst Bakery. The next day Terry appeared on the front page of the Vancouver *Sun*, his head peeking through the toilet seat, his eyes a little out of focus, his happiness apparently complete.

Terry sampled his birthday present, the new leg, the next morning, and after nine miles his stump was raw and bloodied. He broke for a rest and a shower and the steamy water scorched his stump, but he put on his old leg and did another eleven miles. A local reporter spotted the blood and the wire service was alerted.

Terry was flooded with inquiries. Reporters got on the telephone to the War Amputations Association in Ottawa and asked what were Terry's chances of making it. Cliff Chadderton, the association's chief executive, predicted Terry was going to run into "terrible problems" because of the beating inflicted upon the stump.

Terry didn't think anyone had seen the blood. He was used to it. However, he was not used to having alarm bells going off every time he bled. Where was all the concern when he and Doug were alone on the highway in Newfoundland and blood was pouring out of his knee joint? He was angry and belligerent, especially when asked if he would see a doctor.

"I'd see a doctor if I had to, but that depends on what you mean by 'had to.' There's no doctor in the world who's had an amputee who's doing anything on an artificial limb like I am. If I went to see a doctor he'd have a pessimistic approach. What if he did tell me it was okay to keep going and then a week later something happened? Then he'd be in trouble and have to defend himself," he told the *Toronto Star*.

Chadderton said he was disturbed by the reports he was getting from Ontario prosthetists who had examined Terry's stump in Toronto, Hamilton, and London. Terry argued that all of those specialists had told him that his stump was in good condition, considering.

The War Amputations of Canada predicted Terry would soon not be able to tolerate the pain and suggested he should take a breather and consult with a specialist. They were in a delicate position. Said Chadderton: "The guy is so tremendous, but if anyone utters one word of criticism it looks like we're not supporting him. We are worried because the prosthetic reports are coming back to us saying the stump is changing shape, it's developing sores and is not in good condition. He should be seeing an orthopedic man, to check for proper blood flow. The run is very positive and we'd hate to see it abandoned because he's had no medical attention."

But the last word was Terry's. He insisted he knew his own body better than anyone else: "Maybe that's why I've made it as far as I have – 2,521 miles. If I ran to a doctor every time I got a little cyst or abrasion I'd still be in Nova Scotia. Or else I'd never have started. I've seen people in so much pain. The little bit of pain I'm going through is nothing. They can't shut it off, and I can't shut down every time I feel a little sore."

All of this took place on the shore of Lake St. Joseph, near Footes Bay. Terry set off, his ability to heal almost uncanny. To the untrained eye, the tender stump, the cause of all this uproar, seemed to have been only slightly skinned, much as a child's knee is scraped after a sidewalk tumble.

He ran twenty-six miles that day and his parting shot was: "Not bad for a guy who's supposed to be heading for the hospital."

# Chapter Nine

The bleeding-stump episode marked another change for the participants in the Marathon of Hope. Once, shortly afterwards, Doug remembered, Terry, hurting and proud, climbed into the van and said, "Get out. I want to cry alone." Thereafter they allowed him privacy.

Doug was puzzled – was the stump bothering Terry more than he would say? Darrell, who was perhaps more intuitive, sensed that something was wrong. He watched Terry as he ran, and felt each step took too much effort. He lacked the ease and comfort that had marked his stride in New Brunswick and Quebec. Terry's temper had achieved some notoriety, but Darrell felt this new attitude was different. He knew his brother was self-willed and stubborn, but he was not irritable by nature.

Darrell kept looking for reasons, excuses to explain what he saw as a change in Terry. Was it the heat? Was it the hills of northern Ontario that demanded and took much more from Terry? Was it the lack of sleep? Day after day, Terry recorded in his diary that he was waking up exhausted. Puzzled, Doug and Darrell withdrew from Terry just a step. They would be there when he called them, but it seemed that those days he needed to be alone.

Terry had eased out of the crowds that marked southern Ontario. His path along Highway 69 took him along the wild eastern shore of Georgian Bay.

There were good times, too; there had to be, with Terry. In Parry Sound he met Bobby Orr's father, Doug, who presented Terry with "the greatest gift I've ever been given," Bobby's Canada Cup sweater and a large photo of the hockey legend scoring a Stanley Cup winning goal. Terry felt he was in heaven.

Jack Lambert, the paternal Cancer Society district director who accompanied Terry through central Ontario, left the Marathon south of Sudbury. With his round belly and Bermuda shorts, Jack had become a familiar figure on the highway. He had driven hundreds of miles behind Terry at a speed of one or two miles an hour, with his right hand on the wheel, his left hand stretched out the window to receive donations from passersby. His job had been to arrange for local receptions, to make sure volunteers had been stirring up enthusiasm, and, most of all, to make sure that Terry was happy.

Doug characterized Jack as "a man with a heart who backed Terry all the way." Terry responded to that loyalty, and the day Jack left was a sad one. *I'll miss him*, Terry told his diary. *He was great!*

August 4. Terry learned that the van's odometer had been measuring his miles incorrectly and that he had already passed the halfway mark. This was the halfway point of *his* journey, which was quite different from the halfway point of a runner who may have started at Halifax instead of St. John's. The four-per-cent error in the odometer reading allowed them to add an extra sixty-five miles to Terry's total. But Terry refused to regard the blunder as a boon. His pattern of goal-setting – he had been running *towards* the halfway mark for days – was upset. The psychological spark he would receive by crossing the mid-point had been snatched away from him. Terry fell into a funk for a few days, but quickly rallied:

*August 7, near Blind River, Ontario*
*2,734 miles*

*Today was a great day. I finished twenty-six miles by*
*3:20 P.M. First I did fourteen miles then I did twelve. The*
*morning was very cool. In fact, I had to wear a sweater for*
*the first two miles. The miles were strong and solid until the*
*final mile of the day, when I nearly collapsed. Got that*
*empty, weak feeling when the heat and humidity get to me.*
*We are twenty-four miles from Blind River. I met an Indian*
*chief today.*

Terry was to be congratulated on passing the halfway mark for the next 400 miles. It was already a sore point. His fans on the roadside couldn't have known they were testing his patience with their friendly little signs. Terry remembered that "The halfway point really bothered me. I hit halfway just before Sudbury. I get to Sault Ste. Marie and I figure it's all downhill, mileage-wise. I've run more miles than I'll have to for the rest of the trip. I knew what I had done and how it affected me psychologically. Then I see this huge sign: COME ON, TERRY, YOU'RE HALFWAY. LET'S GO ALL THE WAY. Maybe they didn't know what I'd done. Thunder Bay and Sault Ste. Marie have competitions all the time and always argue over who's halfway. Maybe that's why they put the sign up. The first thing I said when I saw that sign was 'I'm more than halfway.' I couldn't wait to get past that sign. In Wawa, maybe Marathon and Nipigon, the official halfway mark, I heard it a lot. There were tiny signs everywhere and I'd stop and actually explain to the people that I'd passed halfway. It was important."

By August 12, Terry had raised $1.4 million and Canadians from Whitehorse to Windsor knew his story. Dorothy Stone of Georgetown started a campaign nominating him for the Order of Canada. She urged Canadians to flood the office of the Secretariat of Honours with the name Terry Fox. Steve Milton, a sports columnist for the Orillia *Packet and Times*, recommended he be named the Canadian Press athlete of the year. The Cancer Society was still boggled by his impact and could scarcely handle the 500 pledges and donations that flooded the Ontario division office daily. Although Terry was a thousand miles away, they were still taking 170 pledges daily and their press officer handled fifty media calls a day.

Terry was also eliciting some concerned comment. "Give It Up, Terry," read a headline in a Peterborough *Examiner* editorial. "It's not a celebration of life to push heroic gesture to the point of self damage . . . if he now deliberately incurs new suffering a thousand hearts made stronger by his example will falter at his folly." Crusty broadcaster Gordon Sinclair called Terry a three-legged horse who should be stopped. And from the Sault *Daily Star*: "Terry Fox has done a magnificent job of rousing the concern of Canadians for others. Now concerned Canadians should implore him to call off his effort before he jeopardizes his entire future."

The worst, by Terry's reckoning, came from the redoubtable *Globe and Mail*, in which he was painted as a tyranical brother, relegating Darrell to the Cinderella role of van-sweeper. The report said he was running because he held a grudge against a doctor who had misdiagnosed his condition back in his locker room days at Simon Fraser. "Trash," Terry grumbled. The clincher was the *Globe*'s quote of the day. The luckless Lou Fine, Jack Lambert's successor, was reported as saying: "It was the society that made the success. He's only doing the running."

That quote bothered Terry least of all. He reasoned that indeed he *was* only doing the running, and that perhaps he hadn't given the society or its corps of volunteers the recognition they deserved. But he was upset when he heard that Fine's job was in jeopardy. Terry announced that if Fine lost his job, he would stop running for the Cancer Society. While the phone jangled at the society offices for a few days, the overall impact of Fine's indiscretion was positive – donations to the Marathon of Hope poured in faster than ever.

What hurt Terry most of all was that he didn't know whom to trust. He saw the Marathon of Hope as a positive force. If reporters were going to write negatively about his efforts, he decided he wouldn't have anything more to do with them. "They missed the point completely," he said. "If they are not positive about the run, I won't talk to them. I'm not here to play games with the media. I don't need all that extra pressure."

The state of his temper was, he felt, not front-page news. Although it was true, as reported, that Darrell had said that Terry sometimes took his frustrations out on him, Terry was annoyed by what the reporter had left out: "He didn't write down the fact that Darrell, at the exact time, also said, 'I don't mind because I know what he's going through. I know what he goes through every day. He's running all day long. I can take it if I have to. If that's going to help him, if it'll help relieve his frustrations, I don't mind.'

"We had good times, too. We went out to dinner and Doug and Darrell and I used to joke and fool around a lot. There were days when I felt good and nobody wrote about that. And it wasn't always me. Darrell and Doug had a fist fight. I don't know if anybody else knows about it. They had a fight about a radio station. Darrell wanted it on and Doug wanted it off, so Doug punched Darrell and Darrell punched him back in the nose and gave him a bleeding nose." Twenty minutes later, Darrell added, they were all laughing about the fracas.

But Terry and Darrell didn't laugh when they read the *Globe* story about their relationship. Months later, Darrell was still bothered by his part. He kept asking himself, "How could I have said that?" Terry told Darrell he couldn't give press interviews anymore. Darrell was hurt. The group decided that only Terry and Doug would speak to reporters. "It bugged me for the rest of the trip," Darrell remembered. "It was one of those things that you look back on and say, 'oh, no.' "

The days continued good and bad. Sometimes the mood of the day depended on whether Terry had been able to sleep the night before. Most nights he couldn't, despite his new home, a twenty-two-foot camper van that had arrived courtesy of General Motors and Jim Pattison Group, a Vancouver car dealer whose name was painted on the van's side.

Terry had become so well known by this time that when a Sault Ste. Marie radio station broadcast that he was stalled because a spring had snapped in his knee, a local welder jumped in his car to make a road call. Within ninety minutes, the spring was repaired and Terry was on the road again.

Terry's brother Fred arrived for his vacation and, just as his parents had in Halifax, took time to help Terry and Darrell sort out their disagreements.

These were also days of triumph for Terry. He had anticipated his run up Montreal River Hill for weeks. The hill was on everyone's mind. Those who knew the hill's reputation had made the three-kilometre slope, south of Wawa, a Goliath to Terry's David. They gave him a T-shirt that read MONTREAL RIVER HERE I COME on one side and I'VE GOT YOU BEAT on the other.

Terry ran four miles before starting the long climb through the romantic landscape, which rises above the deep blue of Lake Superior. He ran the three kilometres without stopping for his usual break. Bill was waiting at the top of the hill. "Is that it?" Terry asked. "That's it," Bill grinned and they slapped hands.

Soon after Montreal River there were two trouble spots on Terry's horizon. He was coughing. It was a light, dry and brittle cough that punctuated his sentences like commas. He would get part way through what he had to say, then he would cough; a few more words and another intruder. It would go away, he knew it would. Then there was the matter of the sore and swollen ankle. He was treating it with an ice pack and continued to run on it.

Inside, he was worried and a little desperate. "Somehow," he told himself, "I think it will go away on its own." His ankle, however, was not as co-operative as his stump had been in healing promptly, on demand. Again he asked himself, "Is it all over?" He worried that he had fractured his foot. He ran on the ankle for three days, although the ice packs no longer masked the pain nor reduced the swelling.

Doug decided to call Ron Calhoun in London to ask for help. Calhoun chartered a twin-engine Aztec and Terry was rushed to hospital in Sault Ste. Marie. He had tendinitis, an inflammation of the tendon and a common affliction among athletes. Terry was given an injection and a handful of pain killers and ordered to stay off his feet for thirty-six hours. The news was a great relief to Terry, who had expected a stress fracture, which would have forced him to stop running for several months. He wrote in his diary that night: *Anxious, waiting, hopeful.*

Terry rested for two days only, then took a bus back to the Marathon to prepare for his next twenty-six miles. He would run a marathon a day for the next four days.

They were glorious days for Terry. The weather was bright and clear; the landscape was all tall timber and deep water, the essence of Canada, and his heart was singing because a little boy, ten years old and hairless as an old man, was riding his bike behind him as he ran. The boy's name was Greg Scott, and like Terry he had bone cancer. Like Terry, he had lost his leg and his hair, but he never lost his hope. The two had met in Hamilton, near Greg's home in Welland, and Terry had questioned Bill nearly every day for news of the pale little boy who, months earlier, was an all-star baseball player.

A family friend, Don Chabot, flew Greg and his parents, Rod and Sharon, to Terrace Bay, a town of 3,000 on the shore of Lake Superior, for the reunion. Greg could do a lot of things Terry couldn't. He could ride a bike. And he could swim better than Terry, who had swum only twice in the three and a half years since he lost his leg.

They tested the water in Jackfish Lake with their artificial legs. "Feels nice," said Terry. "It's warm," said Greg, the *Star* reported.

Christie Blatchford, a reporter from the *Star*, watched from the beach as photographer Boris Spremo clicked away. She watched

Greg hop to the water without his artificial leg and dive in effortlessly. She watched Terry unstrap his own leg and wade towards Greg, who sped to his side squealing and splashing. Terry tumbled off balance into the lake, and the whole Marathon joined in, hooting and whooping its way through the water, just like a bunch of kids on any summer evening. They came out dripping, shirts clinging. The film crew of John Simpson and Scott Hamilton were there, too. Shivering on the beach, Terry found a microphone strapped to his leg and he clucked at John for being devious. Then he picked up his leg and shouted to everyone: "Hey, you guys! You never learned how to walk on an artificial leg, did you? This is how you do it." Then he hopped to the van, his leg in his hand, using it as a cane. Later Terry spoke quietly to Christie Blatchford. He looked around to make sure no one else could hear: "Greg's not as lucky as me. He's got it again. They found a spot of cancer again on his lung."

*Wednesday, August 27, day 138*

*Today I had a good run in the morning. Thirteen miles. The weather was perfect. No wind and cool. In the afternoon my ankle started to hurt again. Greg rode his bike behind me for about six miles and it has to be the most inspirational moment I have had! The final thirteen were hard but I made it! At night we had a beautiful reception in Terrace Bay. I spoke about Greg and couldn't hold back the emotion.*

Terry had become very emotional. He saw the Marathon of Hope as more than a run; he saw it as a great swelling of common purpose among the people of Canada. He was touched beyond words by those who cheered him, supported his cause and shared his dream. He could see it in their faces as he spoke (often as he stood on a picnic table). He was borne along by the crowds. The excitement of the early days, the fund-raising, the message of hope for all cancer patients, all the basic reasons for his run were still strong, but Terry felt something deeper and more profound, which he found difficult to express. He had come close to Canadians through six provinces and sensed that those people, too, wanted to help the world along a little and were inspired by his positve example. He did not want to let anyone down.

*Thursday, August 28, day 139*
*3,255 miles*

*Today was a difficult day. Extremely hilly and I was fatigued.*
*Two film crews were buzzing around me all day. It was a*
*gorgeous day. Beautiful; glorious scenery. I did two*
*interviews at night and then read the Doug Collins [a New*
*Westminster columnist] paper, which said I rode through*
*Quebec and I nearly blew up! Broke my heart! I have a*
*saddened and weakening attitude toward the media and press.*

This is, in part, what Terry read: "God knows, I don't want to
take anything away from Terry Fox, B.C.'s Marathon Man.
Would I spit on the Queen? . . . No, Terry will not have run right
across Canada because he didn't run right across Quebec. And he
didn't run right across Quebec because Quebeckers showed almost
no interest in him . . . he ran only 150 of the 700 miles from Gaspé
Peninsula to Montreal. He did the rest by van, his reception in La
Belle Province being so poor, and then he ran around Montreal to
complete the equivalent mileage."

Terry, who read every word written about him, broke down: "I
read that story when I was fully exhausted and had given everything I had that day in running; then to see that, it just degraded
me and I cried. I burst right down. I punched the wall, and Bill and
the others thought I was going to put a hole through it. It just
burned me, tore through me. To me it was so important to be as
honest as I could, to always tell the truth, and not even to miss a
foot."

Terry phoned New Westminster and a retraction appeared.
"I don't know," he said later, "if I've gotten over it yet."

*Friday, August 29, day 140*
*3,275 miles*

*Today was a difficult day. I didn't sleep last night and was*
*wiped before I started. Exhausted and fatigued all day. Got a*
*lovely, beautiful poem from Rika that lifted my spirits. I feel*
*sick tonight.*

Doug knocked on the cabin door. Terry was soaking the miles
away in a hot bath. Bill was with his family in Welland. Doug

cautiously brought up the matter of Terry's route through Thunder Bay. Lou Fine wanted Terry to run through the city instead of taking a bypass that would save him twelve miles. Terry was worrying about winter. He could already feel the chill in the air. He didn't care about the receptions so much these days. The pressure was on him.

Doug had changed immeasureably since those days in Newfoundland when he would stand still as a post with his arm outstretched with a cup of water. He was Terry's man and he would not let anyone coerce him into running extra miles. "I thought, to hell with those guys," Doug remembered.

As Terry soaked the two old friends chatted. It was a quiet time for them. Terry apologized for being so irritable, as though he couldn't comprehend his own anxiety. Doug, in turn, told Terry that he understood how hard it was. "When I started doing the press work I got a better perception of how difficult it was for Terry and I wasn't even running the miles," Doug said. "Then Terry said he'd probably be bitchy again. But I can't remember if he told me he didn't feel well.

"The next morning it was pouring buckets all through Nipigon. He was sleeping in an extra couple of hours, and it was a good idea because the rain stopped as soon as he came out. He told me he didn't know if he could run because he had the flu. He ran twenty miles that day, Saturday. He wasn't coughing at all.

"The next day, Sunday, he ran twenty-three miles. I told him he had to run fifty-two miles to get to Thunder Bay. There was good weather, and there was no reason he couldn't make twenty-six that day, but he didn't. I thought maybe his foot was still sore."

*Sunday, August 31, day 142*
*3,318 miles*

*Today was all right. Started late and it was cold for the entire morning. Twelve, eleven. Nothing else happened.*

Terry had written the last entry in his diary.

In Terrace Bay, Ontario, Terry frolicked in the water with Greg Scott, like Terry an amputee, who was undergoing chemotherapy at this time.

Throughout his run, Terry suffered from blisters and cysts, but concern for his general health grew only towards the end.

This photograph by Peter Martin won the National Newspaper Award for feature photography.

*TORONTO STAR*

Outside Thunder Bay, Terry admitted he had to stop. Too soon, he and the country were shaken by the news that cancer had spread to his lungs and that he would have to fly home across the miles he had hoped to run.

At the airport in Thunder Bay, Rolly and Betty Fox and Bill Vigars (right) watched as Terry was carried on the private jet that would take him back to British Columbia.

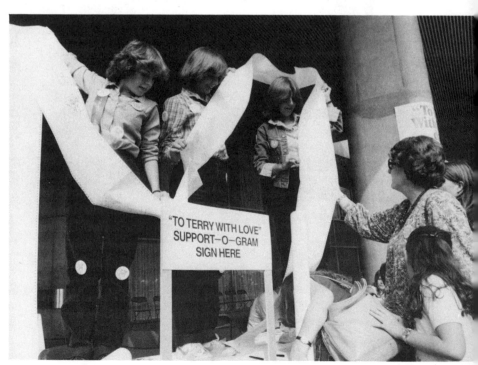

Hundreds of people in Toronto signed the giant scroll, which was later sent to Terry.

CP PHOTO

Betty Fox held her son's hand as he faced the press in Vancouver.

British Columbia Premier Bill Bennett visited Terry's home to present him with the province's highest honour, the Order of the Dogwood.

Governor General Ed Schreyer awarded Terry the Order of Canada in a special ceremony in Port Coquitlam city hall.

Terry's hero, Darryl Sittler of the Toronto Maple Leafs, was one of the many celebrities who took part in CTV's fund-raising television special.

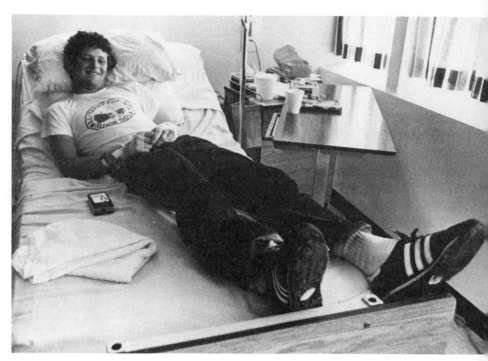

Terry watched the telethon from his bed in the Royal Columbian Hospital in New Westminster, British Columbia, while waiting for his first chemotherapy treatment.

# Chapter Ten

"I had run thirteen miles in the morning and it felt good, it felt real good. It wasn't raining, but it was a cloudy day. Then I ate, as I usually do, and went back to my room – I had a room in a little motel – and slept for a couple of hours. Then I came out and we drove to where I'd left off. By now there were all kinds of people, tons of people, lining the roads waiting for me because the radio stations had been broadcasting.

"I was about eighteen miles out of Thunder Bay. I started running and still felt pretty good. I think it was starting to drizzle rain a little bit. People were clapping me on, cheering me all the way for the whole eight miles that I did in the afternoon. It was super help for me.

"When I finished my fifth mile, I started coughing. I went into the van and I was laying down, taking a drink and a bit of a break. That was my eighteenth mile of the day, or my fifth of that run. I was coughing really hard, and then I felt a pain in my neck that spread into my chest. It was really quite a strong pain. Finally I got myself to quit coughing but the pain didn't leave. I didn't know what to do so I went out and ran because it was the only thing to do. I wasn't going to sit there in the van and wait for it to go away. To me it was like having a blister that I knew would not go away until it had time to heal. As far as I was concerned, the pain in my chest was something that would eventually go away. If it didn't, it would be something that I would have to get checked out.

"People were still lining the road saying to me, 'Keep going, don't give up, you can do it, you can make it, we're all behind you.' Well, you don't hear that and have it go in one ear and out the other, for me, anyways. To me, it goes in one ear and stays there. When I listened to that it meant something to me. Even if I never responded, which I couldn't do all the time, any time anyone said anything to me, I heard. It meant something and probably motivated me.

"Even if I had been by myself, I would have kept going anyway. But I remember that being an important part in the period when I was running – what the people were saying when I had the pain in my chest and it wasn't going away. It was a dull, blunt pain in my upper chest, and it hurt, oh, it really hurt to run, but I kept going, hoping that eventually it would go away or start to fade. After two miles it was getting worse, but my legs were okay and my arms were okay so I could still run. I got those miles done and then I went in the van, took the sleeping bag out and hid in it for fifteen minutes and hoped that by taking that rest it would go away.

"But nothing changed. The pain was still there, so I got up, went out and tried again. There were people lined up for about three-quarters of a mile or so. The van went ahead one mile and waited for me. The police car was behind me. And I was running with this pain in my chest and I began to think, you know, there's something wrong. This may be the last mile.

"There was a camera crew waiting at the three-quarter mile point to film me. I don't think they even realized that they had filmed my last mile. And those comments: people were still saying, 'You can make it all the way, Terry.' I started to think about those comments in that mile, too. Yeah, I thought, this might be my last one.

"I actually thought I had a heart attack. I thought I must have had a slight attack. My breathing hadn't changed; except earlier, the day before, I had noticed a shortness of breath and I thought it was just a cold or something.

"So I ran that mile and got in the van, thinking this might be it. I said to Doug: 'Will you drive me to the hospital? I've got to go and it's not my ankle, it isn't my foot.'

"So we didn't say a word. I just lay there under the covers. Then I told him I didn't want to go into the hospital right away, I wanted a doctor to come and see me in the motel room. So the doctor from the hospital – he was actually from Newfoundland – came out to see me.

"The doctor checked everything. He checked my lungs, too. He told me what he thought it was – either an infection in the lung or a collapsed lung. He was wrong, though.

"I said to him, 'Do you think it might be cancer?'

"He said, 'I don't know. I don't really know at this point, but I don't really think so.'

"Ha, even though he knew, he had asked me, 'When did you have cancer?' and this type of thing. And then I just knew, I knew it, I knew I had it. We went to the hospital and waited.

"I had X-rays and the doctor came into the room and said, 'You've got a slightly collapsed lung. I can't tell if there is an infection or cancer.' But I knew it. I felt shock, incredible, unbelievable shock. How could this happen? Everything was going so great and now, all of a sudden, it's over, the run's over. I can't run any more. The whole thing's changed, now I'm going home.

"Then we went to the doctor's lounge and waited while the doctor went to get the opinion of a specialist. He phoned up a couple of people and got them to come down to the hospital.

"So I said to the doctor again, 'What do you think it is? What do you really think?' and he said again, 'I really don't know.' So we went in to sit down and I cried. I couldn't believe it, I couldn't believe there was any chance of cancer coming back 'cause I'd done all my research and reading. I had gotten to here and now it was all over. That was my intial reaction. Then, like before, I accepted it and realized there wasn't a thing I could do about it and weeping wasn't going to change a thing.

"Even though it wasn't confirmed, I knew I had cancer. Then I went into another room with two doctors. They both said they weren't sure whether there was an infection or cancer. And I said, 'Come on, you've seen this before. You must have an opinion. You've seen the difference before.'

"Then he said to me, 'It looks like it's cancer.' Then I knew for sure.

"That night I phoned my parents. They weren't home so I phoned Mrs. Alward and asked if she could get hold of my parents, tell them to get home so that when I phoned they'd be there. They finally came home and I told my mom, 'Have you heard?' and she said 'Well, I heard on the news that you're sick.' and I said to her, 'No, that's not it. I got cancer in my lungs, cancer again.'

"She broke down right away and Dad got on the phone and he

couldn't believe it either. Right away they said they'd come out. Then Doug Vater – he's an unbelievable person, I don't know where he came from or why he came, but he really helped my parents – he came over, perfect timing, and Mom asked him if he could arrange a plane to Thunder Bay for them. He got to work right away on it. They were going to ask to hold the plane but it would have been for too long a time. So they took the later plane at ten o'clock, and they got out here in the morning. When they came and saw me there wasn't much to be said, really. When they came in, they both grabbed me. We all cried and that was it.

"Even Darrell and Lou Fine didn't know. They had been running around all day looking for me. I thought Doug had got hold of them or somebody had let them know. But I had to tell them, too. They came in the room and I said, 'Did you guys hear?' I was just kind of joking, almost laughing. I had this unbelievable piece of news to give them, and I just said that I got cancer in my lungs again. Darrell said to me, 'Isn't once enough?'

"He and my dad both say things like that. That wasn't my feeling towards it at all. I couldn't feel sorry for myself, or I couldn't get like those people who say it isn't fair. But how can it be fair, when thousands of other people have the same thing? How could I feel sorry for myself when there's little Greg, or somebody else, right now in a hospital, anywhere in the world, dying of cancer? I felt that people all across Canada were going to be seeing me now. I was not gonna be a big ball of tears and feel sorry for myself and say, 'Why me?'

"I decided I was gonna take it as a new change in my life. I was going to have to accept it and fight it, and if there was any way I could, I'd get back out there and run, that's what I was going to do. That's what I said to myself and that's what I said when I was on T.V. too.

"Later I asked the doctor if I could go out to lunch with my parents and Bill – I didn't want to eat in the hospital. He didn't really want me to, but eventually he agreed. We were walking across the road to our car, and all of a sudden I started to feel incredibly terrible and began to get dizzy. I said, 'I can't go out with you. I want to go back to my room.' So I started to walk back across the road. I made it across then I started to get wobbly. Inside the hospital I started to collapse and they grabbed me. There happened to be a chair there and I ended up in it. I had fainted from it all. The day before I had run twenty-six miles and now I couldn't even walk across the road."

That afternoon Terry was carried on a stretcher to Amethyst House, the cancer lodge, and told reporters the news.

"In the press conference it was emotional. I was sitting there and all these people were lined up. I'd come so far. I was nearly two-thirds of the way – and I still don't get recognition for that, damn it – and I'd come through so many hard times, so many different experiences, different weather conditions, times when I couldn't sleep, when the humidity was so bad, and when I had so many things to do at night, times when I nearly got run down. I'd been through so much and I'd made it there. All along I'd said I would never give up, I'd always do my best. I remember saying that when I gave that talk to all the executives, that I was either going to make it or not going to make it. I remembered saying people can live with cancer or can die with cancer and still be winners. I'm sure I said it that time, too, that either way, in this run, I was going to turn out a winner, because I'm either going to make it or if I don't it's because something happened that I can't do anything about. That is exactly what happened and so I felt like I had won. I felt like I had made it, even though I hadn't. And a lot of people told me that, too.

"I knew I could have done the last 2,000 miles, if I had the chance. I knew that myself and that helped.

"But at the press conference, they were respectful. They weren't scared to ask questions, but they let me talk and say my own piece to begin with. I was surprised they didn't ask more than they did. I think it was because of respect for the situation I was in, with my parents there, too. I think it showed class, for the media, anyway."

As he spoke, Betty and Rolly were by his side. Betty held Terry's hand. In her other hand she held a tissue. She was forever wiping her eyes dry. Tears streamed down her pale cheeks. All the lines in her face, around her eyes, those beneath her mouth curved bitterly downward. Rolly's eyes were hard, his mouth taut and grim. They listened as Terry spoke to the sorrowful band of reporters.

"Well, you know, I had primary cancer in my knee three and a half years ago, and now the cancer is in my lungs and I have to go home" – his voice fractured into brittle bits as he spoke, but he picked up the pieces and continued, his voice softer than ever –

"and have some more X-rays and maybe an operation that will involve opening up my chest or more drugs. I'll do everything I can. ᴸ I'm gonna do my very best. I'll fight. I promise I won't give up."

Christie Blatchford was there, flown in on a Lear jet by the *Toronto Star*. She jumped in the ambulance with the Fox family to hear Rolly say:

"I think it's unfair. Very unfair."

"I don't feel this is unfair," Terry replied. "That's the thing about cancer. I'm not the only one. It happens all the time, to other people. I'm not special. This just intensifies what I did. It gives it more meaning. It'll inspire more people. I could have sat on my rear end, I could have forgotten what I'd seen in the hospital, but I didn't.

"How many people do something they really believe in? I just wish people would realize that anything's possible if you try, dreams are made if people try. When I started this run, I said that if we all gave one dollar, we'd have $22 million for cancer research, and I don't care, man, there's no reason that isn't possible. No reason. I'd like to see everybody go kind of wild, inspired with the fund-raising."

Then Terry closed his eyes. The ambulance arrived at the airport where a private Lear jet was waiting to whisk him across the prairies, the Rocky Mountains, and the British Columbia coastal range to Vancouver and the Royal Columbian Hospital. The Ontario Ministry of Health arranged for the charter, which would be paid for by the British Columbia medical plan. There had been talk of using the *Star*'s chartered jet to take Terry home, but it would have cost thousands of dollars and could have gone only as far as Winnipeg.

Terry, still strapped in a stretcher, was loaded onto the little jet. There was room only for his parents and Dr. Geoffrey Davis, a Cancer Society medical advisor. There was an alarming build-up of fluid in Terry's lungs, and the doctor was prepared to drain the fluid or order an emergency landing if Terry couldn't be cared for in the air. Bill Vigars was left desolate on the tarmac. He had been in Welland celebrating his parents' fortieth wedding anniversary and had rushed to Thunder Bay as soon as Lou Fine had called with the news that Terry didn't had the flu, as had been initially reported, but that he had cancer. They had hugged good-bye, and

Terry realized in that sturdy embrace how very much he loved Bill and what good a friend he had become.

Over the lakes of Manitoba, the wheatfields of Saskatchewan, the foothills of Alberta, the magnificent snowy peaks of British Columbia, the 2,000 miles he believed he would run, Terry drifted in and out of sleep. Betty wept and chatted with Dr. Davis, reminiscing about Terry's youth and the exceptional amount of drive he had always shown. She said she had always been afraid of this day. Terry thought and thought. In the scenarios he created in his mind, he had sometimes fantasized about the one where the cancer spread to his lungs two months *after* he finished running. Never in his most desperate moments had he considered it would recur while he was running. In fact, he had asked Dr. Davis if he couldn't stay in Thunder Bay, take treatment, and then continue running. He wanted to finish his Marathon, secondary cancer or not. When the doctor explained he was too ill to carry on, Terry accepted and understood that he had to go home. He was in a great deal of pain.

In Vancouver, a corps of reporters and cameramen waited for the plane to touch down at a small airstrip across the highway from the international airport. At the last moment, hoping to protect Terry from prying cameras and questions, Dr. Michael Piper had requested that the aircraft land at an alternate runway.

Darrell and Doug, meanwhile, were in a commercial airplane, coming home alone. Both felt they had been deprived of the final moments. Both wanted to be with Terry until the last words were spoken at a press conference.

"After being so together for four and a half months, all of a sudden being snapped apart was difficult," Doug recalled. "I wanted to be there until the end. It wasn't really over. We had to get on an airplane before it was all finished."

In the air, Darrell kept peppering Doug with the same question: "What are you going to do?" Neither had an answer. Their lives had been bound up in Terry's – his food, his clothing, his water breaks, his speeches, his moods, and his need for them – and now they were adrift, flying to an uncertain future.

Terry, who had always been generous with the media, continued to be, despite the throbbing in his lungs. At the hospital, Dr. Ladislav Antonik, the Royal Columbian's medical director, herded the reporters into a basement room to wait. Terry arrived in a crowded elevator. He was sitting in a wheelchair but at the door to the press conference, pride pushed him to his feet and he walked in.

He said he would like to finish the run, maybe next year or the year after. He learned that Darryl Sittler was ready to organize the Toronto Maple Leaf hockey team and the National Hockey League players' association to collect pledges and finish the last 2,000 miles for Terry. "No, thanks," he said. He wanted to do it himself.

He said he wasn't disappointed in himself for not finishing this time. He said he was happy with what he had done. If he felt any bitterness it was because some business people had tried to use him to sell their products, but he didn't elaborate.

Betty, still by his side, still holding his hand, was asked how she felt. She was mute. She struggled to speak, and realized she couldn't. Rolly helped her out: "We've been through this before."

Upstairs, his friends Rick Hansen, Peter Colistro, and Rika Noda were waiting for him. Pia Shandel, a host for "The Vancouver Show," had been following Terry from the beginning and was allowed into his room for a few moments. I was there, too, thinking of our mingled destinies, wishing it was as easy to be a reporter as to be a friend. I was vacationing in Vancouver with my husband, Paul, and our family, and had been in touch with the *Star* all day about Terry. Mary Deanne Shears, the city editor, had phoned early telling me Terry was sick, and on his way home, and that I was to cover the press conference. We had been planning to go back-packing in Garibaldi Provincial Park for a few days but had held off that morning because of the rain. Now we waited for Terry.

I had moped around the house all that day, flipping dials on the radio to hear the latest word from Thunder Bay. I wept in confusion, feeling perhaps as Rolly did, that it was unjust. I puzzled, too, about God's curious plans, and I wondered how Terry, ever the optimist, would wrestle with his new destiny.

And at the end of the day, I was standing on the sidelines again, this time in his hospital room watching and listening as Terry set the tone by congratulating Rick and Peter on another championship-winning wheelchair basketball season.

It seemed we all dreaded speaking of cancer; as though, by saying the word, the disease would become more entrenched. So Terry talked about it: "I'm facing it. I'm taking one day at a time. I'm keeping up hope. I'm being positive. I don't want people in here feeling sorry for me. I'm going to be as strong as I can and maybe even get out and do things. I'm hoping the lung condition will improve."

Then he said: "It's one thing to run across Canada, but now people are really going to know what cancer is."

He knew that we had become wrapped up in him as a personality and forgotten about cancer. While he said he figured he had the beast licked, he had never really forgotten that cancer had changed his life and given him a new purpose. Most people didn't remember that. They saw Terry as the Marathon of Hope. They donated because they saw an audaciously healthy kid with one leg and, as the song written for him said, the heart of a lion.

While struggling to find purpose in why he was struck twice, Terry realized that the millions of Canadians who had been calling him a hero would now see cancer as the nasty-natured and pernicious disease that it was. Perhaps now the fund-raising would go wild, as he hoped. It was September 2 and he had raised $1.7 million – far short of his dream of one dollar from every Canadian. The way he saw it, the Marathon of Hope wasn't ending. The real marathon, that long race for his life and the true test of his hope, was beginning.

# Chapter Eleven

Terry wore his Marathon of Hope T-shirt – his favourite one with the map of Canada and the maple leaf on it – through his first weeks in hospital. He wore jeans and sneakers, too, as if defying his tragedy. He saw visitors selectively. His eyes stayed hard and sullen. Sometimes he'd never look up, but would keep his gaze fixed on a six-inch stack of mail – much of it on gingham or pastel-coloured stationery – and talk without enthusiasm about taking one day at a time and being tired. When he did look into your eyes, perhaps with a farewell handshake, there was such fierceness and desperation that words seemed unnecessary. That was Terry's period of adjustment. A week before he had been healthy, his world limitless, and his future in his own hands. Already the brilliant slashes of sunburn across his cheekbones were starting to fade, replaced by rings of weariness.

The diagnosis was grim. The tumours had spread, metastasized, to both lungs: in the right was a well-defined tumour, the size of a golf ball; in the left, an amorphous, fist-sized shape. It was difficult to know the exact size of the left tumour, which appeared as a haziness on the X-rays, because it was surrounded by so much fluid.

Tests – in which cells were removed from the tumour by inserting a hollow needle into Terry's chest – revealed calcium in the tumour, a sure sign that the malignant cells had spread from Terry's knee. Since osteogenic sarcoma often tends to lodge in the liver and in the bones, Terry was given a computerized body scan and a bone scan to see if the disease had spread. Apparently it hadn't.

Doctors had to explain to reporters, who passed it on to the

162

public, that Terry did not have lung cancer, which is usually a disease of the elderly. It was sometimes difficult to understand that Terry had malignant bone cells growing in his lungs. It was reported he had a 10-per-cent chance of beating the disease.

It had taken a somewhat longer than average time for the malignancy to spread. Most metastases occur within eighteen months to two years of primary cancer, although recurrence is sometimes delayed if chemotherapy is used following surgery. It is not known whether those cells lay dormant in Terry's lungs for three and a half years, or had been slowly growing all the time. Terry's doctor believed the tumours would have been visible in chest X-rays about five months before, although they would have still been very small.

Dr. Michael Noble, a cancer specialist, was in charge of the case. He came from a well-known medical family. His father, Dr. Robert Noble, was the researcher who developed the cancer drug vincaleukoblastine, an alkaloid derived from the periwinkle plant, which produced dramatic results in childhood leukemias and Hodgkin's disease.

The tumour in Terry's left lung was too large and parts of it extended too close to his heart for all the cells to be cleanly removed surgically. Terry had to face chemotherapy again. The question was: what drug could he take? He already had a lifetime dose of adriamycin. If he took any more, the risk of heart damage would be increased. Methotrexate was ruled out because of the fluid in Terry's lungs. The drug tends to pool in fluids, and there was a danger it could be released unpredictably and possibly be re-absorbed by the blood stream.

The alternative was a relatively new drug, cis-platinum, which had been licensed for only one year and which didn't have the same side-effects as adriamycin and Methotrexate, but which did cause unprecedented nausea. Terry was given the drug intravenously, preceded by a saline solution to maintain a high urine output, because there was danger that the platinum could cause heavy-metal poisoning of his kidneys.

The first Sunday in September, Terry lay fully dressed watching the fluids drain from the bottles hanging above his hospital bed into his veins. It was the start of his first chemotherapy treatment and he was rooting for the cancer drugs. He was looking at television, as well, watching, in considerable disbelief, John Denver, who had taped a song especially for him. He saw other popular singers: Elton John, Glenn Campbell, Anne Murray, and Nana Mouskouri, all singing for him. There was Karen Kain, who risked her beautiful neck dancing on a concrete floor for him. She slipped once and carried on magnificently.

Terry drifted in and out of sleep. He saw Darryl Sittler, Paul Williams, Gordon Lightfoot, and Ken Taylor, Canada's former ambassador to Iran, not to mention the whole troupe from the Stratford Festival's "Beggar's Opera." There were the premiers of the ten provinces, stopping en route to the first and ill-fated constitutional conference, all praising him.

It was the CTV network's tribute to Terry Fox, five hours of prime Sunday time with local hook-ups from coast to coast, organized, remarkably, in less than forty-eight hours. Terry saw, in the background of the Toronto studios, blown-up posters of himself, the famous one where he is huge and brawny, running on a wet highway on the west coast. There was also a big tote board that jumped, according to one report, $25,000 a minute.

Terry's excitement was ingenuous: "John Denver's doing that for me?" It seemed that the people of Canada had taken over where Terry had left off. As CTV president Murray Chercover said, Terry would see that his "torch will be held."

Terry fell asleep during the broadcast, but later saw the entire show on video-tapes. Darrell was with Terry during the show. "I got the sense he felt so helpless. Those drugs were going through him and there was nothing he could do. Sometimes I wished I could help, but I felt fortunate to be there with him."

By the end of the CTV broadcast, there was $10.5 million in the Terry Fox Fund. One million dollars came from the British Columbia government for an institute founded in Terry's name as part of the province's Cancer Research Centre. Ontario announced that a one-million-dollar endowment fund in Terry's honour would be given to the Ontario Cancer Treatment and Research Foundation. Some big chunks came from corporations: Imperial Oil's president Jim Livingstone donated $100,000 on air. Others, including McDonald's of Canada, Coca-Cola Ltd., Shell Canada, and Standard Brands, also gave generously. The rest came from the people. September became Terry Fox month in communities across Canada.

A couple of teenagers walked through Toronto's old money

neighbourhood, Forest Hill, and collected $600 for Terry in one afternoon. At Simon Fraser University, faculty and staff raised $4,500 in one hour, and the university struck a gold medal in his honour and established a $1,000 scholarship to be awarded to a student showing "courage in adversity and dedication to society."

Students from Cloverdale Catholic School in British Columbia held a boot throw to raise money. In Quebec City, a bank-robber-turned-disc-jockey organized a twenty-kilometre march for him. In Kelowna, British Columbia, the Woodlake Old Time Fiddlers held a dance. In Newfoundland, a man offered to skate 2,000 miles for Terry. A Montreal pianist offered to hold a Chopin recital. There were walk-a-thons, run-a-thons, stitch-a-thons (stitch a quilt in a bank in Oakville, Ontario, and donate one dollar) and cut-a-thons. Toronto businessmen who organized a To-Terry-With-Love day and filled Nathan Phillips Square with admirers in a bittersweet day of nostalgia raised $40,000. Ontario strippers reduced to their G-strings for Terry, which caused some raised eyebrows at the Cancer Society and some murmurs about maintaining standards of taste. And in Port Coquitlam, two six-year-olds, Tara Binder and Melanie Ward, sold cold drinks behind a little sign that said HAVE A LEMONADE AND HELP TERRY HELP THE WORLD.

The magnificent outpouring came not just from Canada, but from around the world. Letters arrived from Saudi Arabia and Israel, from Ireland and Malaysia, even from a family of United Church missionaries in Nepal. Terry received hundreds of thousands of letters, some merely addressed: *Terry Fox, General Delivery, Canada*. Some letters urged him to try unusual herbal remedies, including a grape cure; others urged him to use his influence to stop the use of animals in cancer research. The post office said he received more mail than the entire city of Port Coquitlam during the Christmas season. Bobby Orr and his wife, Peggy, flew to Vancouver and had dinner at home with Terry and his family. Douglas Bader, the RCAF hero who lost both legs in the Second World War, wrote Terry, as did Senator Edward Kennedy. Prime Minister Trudeau sent a telegram: "I was distressed indeed to hear that you are again engaged in a fight with your old enemy . . . the whole country is pulling for you." Later that month, Governor General Ed Schreyer flew to Port Coquitlam to make Terry the youngest Companion of the Order of Canada in a special ceremony. Terry enjoyed it but wished, as always, he could have been given credit for running nearly two-thirds of the way across Canada, instead of half.

Later, British Columbia Premier Bill Bennett came up to the Fox house and awarded Terry the Order of the Dogwood, the province's highest honour.

Terry was bombarded with accolades. So many, in fact, that some were stacked in a pile against a living-room wall. The gifts that were most prominently displayed, for a time, were the blow-up of the famous photograph of Bobby Orr flying through the air after scoring an overtime goal to win the 1970 Stanley Cup and, more permanently, a close-to-life-size double portrait of Terry. The painting, which was so large it could be seen by passersby on the street, was done from news photographs by a local admirer. Terry was also named Canadian Press newsmaker of the year and was given the Lou Marsh trophy for his outstanding athletic achievement. That pleased Terry as much as any of the other honours, for all his life he had sought athletic accomplishments, no matter if he had one leg or two. "If what I did isn't an athletic achievement, what is?" Terry asked. He was glad, as well, that the athletic aspect of his run had been recognized. Later his portrait was permanently enshrined in the Canadian Sports Hall of Fame.

Those months were the best and worst for Terry. As he told the Vancouver *Sun*: "Both things were going on. One was so fantastically great and positive and the other was about as terrible as you can get." The fund-raising, the letters, the cards, the poems, all helped Terry's spirits immeasurably. However, the cis-platinum was not doing so well against the cancer. There seemed to be no improvement. In fact, Dr. Noble said the tumours looked worse. Terry felt a lot of pain in his left side. When he spoke, there was an obvious shortness of breath.

Since there appeared to be less fluid in his lungs, Dr. Noble started him on aggressive Methotrexate treatment again, once a week, instead of every three weeks. After the second treatment, Terry lapsed into a nightmarish world of hallucination and pain, what Dr. Noble called "the episode of confusion." Terry did not eat for three weeks. His mouth and throat were sore with cankers, a condition known as mucositis. He lost between fifteen and twenty pounds.

166

"I couldn't walk. I was watching television and Mom had to come help me to bed. I was so weak, my bones were next to nothing. I felt I had some kind of reaction in my head. Dr. Heffelfinger came and asked a thing or two. He tried to force me to drink. I just couldn't. Then he gave me an injection of some sort that put me out. The next morning I woke up and I didn't know what was going on. Mom and Dad said, 'We really can't help you there. You may as well go to a hospital.' They called an ambulance to take me in. Mom didn't think I was coming home again. They put things on me to help me breathe on the way there.

"That night was the worst of my life. I was hallucinating. I didn't know what room I was in. It was awful, a nightmare, but I was awake. I couldn't explain it. It was just that this terrible thing was happening. It finally got dark. I'd see a nurse every now and then, just to make sure it was all real, that everything was okay. Mentally I was just lost.

"They did a brain scan, but there was nothing wrong. They parked me out in the hall, waiting for someone to take me to my room. I was lying there all by myself and started thinking, What's going on? I looked at myself, at my left leg and the size of my right leg – you know how big my leg was. I thought, Is this it? Am I here for good now? Then I started to remember. I decided I was bored there. There was nothing seriously wrong and I was okay. The lung doctor had told me the tumour in my right lung had shrunk and the left lung hadn't changed, so there shouldn't be anything different. When Dr. Noble checked me I told him I wanted to go home, and he said okay. They got a wheelchair for me and I could barely get into it. Dad had to push it.

"I had decided. It was a change in mental attitude, deciding I was going back to where I had been before, that I would fight it as best I could. I wasn't going to let it take me that easily."

Terry's toughness had won another battle.

Dr. Noble said the reaction was a side effect to the combination of cancer drugs, pain killers, and an anti-nausea drug, as well as the incredible stress of being Terry Fox. They adjusted the drug dosage and cut back the treatment, and Terry responded well for a month. The right tumour shrank even more.

Terry took advantage of the time to put his house in order. He started with simple things, such as cleaning up his room, which was filled with souvenirs of his trip. Terry appeared in educational films for the Cancer Society and was paid for his work. The man who had by that time raised $18.5 million for cancer research was flat broke, and wondered how he would pay for Christmas presents. He gave interviews until he exhausted himself, but he had a lot to say. In a revealing series of stories for the Vancouver *Sun*, Terry acknowledged his own carelessness in failing to have regular check-ups, and he gave reporters unusual access to his doctors. The result was spellbinding reading. He also spoke of his faith, and admitted it was difficult to tell a roomful of reporters that he believed in God.

He told me he still felt he was "in the woods" and wanted to become closer to God: "I think of the world and what's going on. Because man's gone through history with so much death, killing, stealing, I don't think man can do it on his own. It's obvious what's going to happen on this earth unless man changes. I, for one, need something to grab onto, to hold onto. I haven't been told I'm going to die of cancer. When that happens, I want to have so much faith I won't have any fears at all. At the press conference in Thunder Bay the last question was: 'Is Terry Fox afraid?' Of course, I'm afraid. You'd be afraid, too, if you were in my position. Now, if my doctor tells me I'm going to die, I want to be able to say I'm not afraid."

Terry had fun in those months, too. Sometimes he joined Rick Hansen and his basketball buddies for an evening at a Port Coquitlam pub. One night Terry was asked for I.D. The waitress gasped when she saw his name. Moments later a free round of drinks arrived at the table. Terry, forgetful of his fame, asked ingenuously, "Why are they giving us free beer?"

He still dreamed of running: "I believe that God planned what happened. There was a reason for what happened to me in Thunder Bay. Right now I'm going to fight as hard as I can to beat cancer. If I do, if I come back from this and finish running across Canada, it will be the greatest comeback I ever made."

Terry started testing himself again. One day he drove up to Westwood Mountain to the go-cart track where he had trained the year before. He had looked at his pitifully thin leg and decided to make it strong again. He started walking. The track was a big loop with cut-off points along the way, so he could either complete the quarter-mile circuit or cut off at any of the loops. He was weak, "almost falling over," at the first cut-off, but he insisted on completing the circuit. "I had to go all the way around. That's just the way I am about everything. It's things like that that I love. They challenge me. They inspire me."

Terry had other challenges, too. No matter how much he talked about religion and becoming a better person, he was still cantankerous on the home front. Betty, who had left the card shop, was usually on the firing line, coping with his snappishness. She was careful to gauge his mood before asking him a question. "When Terry gets angry, it's me that gets it," she said matter of factly. "And when there are other people around, he cuts everyone else out." Remembering what Lou Fine once said in a *Globe and Mail* interview, Betty added, "I could see people getting mad at Terry to the point of punching him in the nose."

Terry was aware of his wilful temperament. It was ironic, yet an insight into his ultimately high-minded nature, that just as he fought cancer, he tried to tame his stormy personality. He tried very hard to improve, but it was tough battling his own instincts and upbringing.

Betty was a Kleenex away from tears most of the time, but, as she said, "When you're around Terry, you have to be strong." Terry's stubbornness was only a small part of the problem because, more than anything, Betty believed her family had been dealt too many unfair blows – first her brother Fred lost his legs, her sister Norma was killed in a car accident, and now Terry. Considering all of that, Betty was remarkably controlled and the focus of strength in the family. Among the few people she could turn to for support was Alison Sinson, an assistant director of nursing at the Royal Columbian Hospital, and Lynn Bryan, an administrative assistant at the Cancer Society.

She slept on the couch to be closer to Terry's room so she could hear him if he needed her. If he couldn't sleep they'd stay up together. "Thank God for all-night television," she'd say. Rolly was back at work. The fellows in the railroad yard had rallied and each worked a day for him so that he could have a few weeks off when Terry first came home from Thunder Bay.

Others felt the strain, too. There were many requests for Darrell to appear at fund-raising events on Terry's behalf. He wanted to participate, but Betty kept him at home, saying that if he went to one benefit he'd have to go to them all. Eventually Darrell took a part-time job for a janitorial company to save money for a car and tuition at Simon Fraser University. Betty had convinced him, too, to take on an academic challenge.

Doug gave many interviews over the next three months. He still wore the familiar grey track suit from the Marathon of Hope and carried a terrible burden. He confessed he felt guilty about Terry's illness, as though he were somehow responsible: "I sometimes wonder if I helped cause his cancer. Sometimes stress, emotion, diet can cause it. He didn't have a relapse for three and a half years. I was there those last four months when it recurred. Subconsciously I reacted to him and made him stressful." In the new year Doug moved out of his parents' home and returned, somewhat unhappily, to Simon Fraser University.

Bill Vigars had difficulty adjusting to his job for several months. He took long lunches and often broke down and cried about Terry. Like Doug, he felt lost. Both had been snapped away so suddenly. Bill still kept Terry's T-shirt and shorts from the last mile, and he had one of Terry's running shoes in his desk drawer. He tried to convince the Ford Motor Company not to sell the Marathon of Hope van. He kept a tape recorder nearby to play songs that Terry had liked. One of Bill's favourite was Willie Nelson's country and western hit "On the Road Again." "That's Terry and me," Bill said. One night when the office emptied he sobbed, "I don't want him to die."

I moped around the *Star* for a couple of months. At night I dreamed of Terry. Sometimes the dreams were uplifting, sometimes frightening. Once, after I'd read of the stress of chemotherapy, I dreamed Terry said: "You've got to help get me out of here."

Everyone, close to Terry or far away, felt helpless.

The family showed the stuff they were made of, particularly at Christmas. They had never seen so many presents under the tree. They held their usual Christmas Eve open house. The dining-room table was laden with Nanaimo bars, shortbreads, and homemade fudge, the handiwork of Betty's mother, Mary Ann Wark. Terry, his skin the colour of porcelain, his features more refined and childlike than ever, sat in the big, comfortable, colonial-style chair, mostly watching, sometimes talking quietly to family friends who sat in a circle of chairs in the living room. His intensity, which positively radiated, contrasted with the gaiety around him. Someone told Betty and Rolly they looked well. "Do I?" said Betty, curling her stockinged feet. "Do I?" said Rolly, sceptically. The strain was evident. A friend brought in a two-foot-high bottle of Canadian Club, gay with ribbons. It had been passed around the Christmas Eve circle for eight years and was to be retired that season. When it was Terry's turn to drink from the bottle, the Polaroid and Instamatic cameras flashed. "Ah, ha," joked Betty's best friend, "I'm going to sell this to the Vancouver *Sun* and people will see what the *real* Terry Fox is like." The laughter was welcomed.

Terry was coughing again that night. He wondered if it was a cold or cancer. When the jokes got raucous and the bottle circulated for the second time, Terry left his seat and walked slowly down the hall as if in pain. He had already started unbuttoning his shirt. Without saying good-night, he walked into his room and closed the door.

Terry had eight chemotherapy treatments between September and January. His goal was always to get out of hospital and home as soon as possible. Dr. Noble said Terry was a perfect patient, except for one fault: he would say he was feeling fine and was well enough to go home even while throwing up. The doctor noticed that patients with positive attitudes tended to handle the chemotherapy better.

After the treatment in the last week of January, Betty moved a little cot into Terry's hospital room so she could be with him day and night. His condition was worsening. The next week, Dr. Antonik announced in a press conference from the Royal Columbian Hospital that chemotherapy was not working and that tumours had spread first to Terry's abdomen, then to the lymph glands surrounding the aorta, the artery that distributes blood to most parts of the body. This time Terry and his parents did not face the press.

Interferon, a rare and costly natural substance extracted from living cells, was the only alternate course of treatment although its effectiveness against osteogenic sarcoma was still inconclusive. Isadore Sharp, Terry's long-time benefactor, told the national office of the Cancer Society of the Denver, Colorado, outlet where the interferon (which was produced in Philadelphia) was available. The society sent an initial deposit of $15,000 – though it wasn't known how much the overall treatment would cost, since doctors were experimenting with dosages – and a few days later, Terry received his first injection of human fibroblast interferon, derived from cells in the connective tissue. The substance was flown to the Royal Columbian where Terry was treated as an out-patient, his parents always by his side. At first, it was reported that only a miracle could save Terry, and all the people of Canada started praying for that miracle. Letters-to-the-editor pages were dotted with requests for days of prayer and fasting in Terry's honour. He was sent home, with an intravenous feeder and around-the-clock private nursing.

Cancer patients were devasted by the news of his set-back, and struck by the irony that the man who had raised millions in aid of cancer research could not benefit from his own labour. Terry had been their model of hope, and it seemed they had been cut adrift again. To some, the slogan "Cancer can be beaten" seemed bitterly inappropriate. For others, Terry had taken the mystery out of the disease – at least the public knew cancer wasn't contagious – and they were deeply grateful.

Terry continued to balance on the edge of two futures: he could die, or he could recover and finish running. While he accepted the first, he prayed for the second. He saw Rika occasionally and kept reading the New Testament. He prayed. He continued to be stubborn, and that was a pleasing quality, considering he was so very ill. The tumours pressed against his abdomen and he retched frequently. He played cards, watched television, was given morphine to kill the pain. He saw his friends and went to matinees when he felt strong.

The interferon treatment was not successful. Terry suffered an adverse reaction and returned to the hospital in late February. He had surgery to relieve the pressure on his heart, and reporters kept a vigil in the lobby, anticipating the worst. No one counted on Terry's great strength. He went home again and rested, watched hockey games on television, and once saw a banner that read: KEEP ON FIGHTING, TERRY FOX, strung along the stands.

While he meditated on his future, Canadians considered his legacy. More than $23.4 million had been raised; he had realized his dream of one dollar from every Canadian. He had more than doubled the National Cancer Institute of Canada's 1980 research allowance of $15.6 million. The money Terry raised was chanelled into several research areas, including the Terry Fox Special In-itiatives program, which allowed grants of up to one million dollars each for two top cancer researchers; the Terry Fox Training Centre Establishment Grants, designed to attract promising young researchers; and the Terry Fox Special Cancer Research Fund, which would administer grants of up to $150,000 to Canada's medical and science faculties to intensify their on-going cancer research programs. The fund was administered by the National Cancer Institute and the Canadian Cancer Society.

Shortly after the interferon treatment failed, the province of British Columbia announced plans to honour Terry further by constructing a $25 million interferon plant in Vancouver. Interferon could then be produced and supplied on a non-profit basis across Canada.

But the gift he left most of us was not measured in dollars.

Having seen him, we knew something of courage and compassion. To some he became a symbol of unity, and he spurred a heart-thumping national pride. Politicians debating the patriation of the BNA Act or the price of Canadian oil were berated by their constituents for not being able to bring the country together the way Terry had. Perhaps it was because Terry had crossed the nation with a maple leaf on his chest, and had spoken, openly of being a proud Canadian.

The simplicity of his dream fascinated us. It was the dream of a young man, innocent enough to believe he could make the world a better place, wise enough to do it modestly. Although, according to George Woodcock, Canadians "suspect the sheer gigantic irrationalism of the heroic, for we like to consider ourselves a reasonable people," we made Terry a hero. We did that because he met the requirements of heroism: he had made our world a finer place by his presence and he had sacrificed himself for a cause. Though his obsession may have struck some as being irrational, there was little of the giant about him – except, perhaps, the vastness of his dream. We felt comfortable accepting Terry as a hero because he was ordinary enough for us to see something of ourselves in his struggle. It would be nice to think that our own wills could triumph over adversity as Terry's had.

Terry was refreshing, too, because he represented old-fashioned values at a time when most of us had had enough of modern narcissism and indulgence. Duty, dedication, and honour – qualities more fitting to Victorian than contemporary social values – were his trademark. Perhaps that's why Terry was such a welcomed phenomenon in the summer of 1980. His heroism was within our reach, and any of us – old or young, rich or poor, successful or struggling – could aspire to the attitude of excellence he displayed.

Through it all – from the isolation in the bleak hills of New-foundland to the uproar in southern Ontario – Terry remained guileless. Yet he had heart enough to weep, without shame, when a little girl, a cancer victim like himself, honoured him with a spring flower.

Terry started his run with the excitement and energy of a young colt. He wanted to raise money, he wanted to inspire cancer pa-tients. But as he ran, he became more thoughtful. He saw a greater meaning in his struggle, one that could be applied to the healthy as well as the sick. So it was that, in time, whatever Terry was prov-ing to himself took a backseat to what he was proving to everyone else. He made it clear that although the individual had fared badly in our era, one person, any man or woman, could make a dif-ference. He didn't have to be especially gifted; he could be as or-dinary as the boy who worked hard to make the Mary Hill Cobras basketball team. All he needed was the will.

Terry knew he was setting an example, and in time he himself became elevated by the message he delivered with each step: Every individual is important. Just look at what one man can do. People looked at Terry and then at themselves and asked: Have I done my best? Have I made a contribution? Have I lost a dream?

He observed that many of us felt helpless, that our voices weren't heard, that we felt we couldn't control our own destinies. Terry believed we could. As a cancer patient he refused to take his loss mildly. His leg was gone, but his fighting spirit was alive and kicking. Not forgetting the suffering he had seen in the cancer wards, he pushed himself 3,339 miles to prove the dominance of his will and to pay back the debt. What ultimately excited him was the sight of other Canadians sharing his dream: "I believed those people wanted this world to be a better world, and they really tried, they all contributed."

Terry was uncommonly blessed with hope. He refused to be humbled by the disease burgeoning inside him. Even if cancer did claim him, Terry believed he was still a winner. There was no other way he could look at his life. In twenty-two years, he had contributed more – materially and spiritually – than many who live to a gentle old age. Terry wouldn't want us to weep for him; he'd want us to hear his message and be uplifted.

# Epilogue

"I don't care what percentages the doctor tells me I have. If God is true I know I've got 100 per cent, if that's what He has in His plans for me. And if I really believe and if God is really there, then I'm not going to lose even if I die, because it's supposed to be the Pearly Gates I'm going through, and if heaven is there, I can't lose out.

"It's something I have to have a lot of faith in, and I've got to be as strong as I can and I've got to believe it. The situation I'm in right now, I could be down, I could be depressed, I could be out of it, I could be feeling sorry for myself, all of this, but I've got to have hope.

"It's all an attitude, whatever your situation in life. I could be bitter but I can't be that way, because even if I only have two months to live I want to live those two months as best as I can, as healthy as I can, as happy as I can. I don't want to be upsetting other people by my depression. I want to help them as much as I can. I know it's hard on my parents, it's hard on my brothers. I often wonder, how is Judy doing? She goes to school, and at home her brother has a reaction and he's in bed, he's wiped out. It's probably harder on them than it is on me, because I can do something about it. I'm able to fight it and they probably don't understand as much as I do that I *can* do it.

"This is where we're really talking about life. Like Doug. He phoned Rika and said, 'You know, I'm praying for Terry and he doesn't seem to be getting any better. What's going on?' When I heard that, it just made me feel great because of the thought that he was doing that for me. Now we're really talking about what's keeping me going. Through my whole run I thought about the meaning of life. I thought about so many things. I realized that wealth is nothing, because I haven't got any wealth and that didn't make any difference to me. Fame? I've become famous; it hasn't changed my life, and yet you know that's what people right now spend their whole lives striving for.

"On my run, when I got emotional, it was because I was happy, it was a life-happening, like that girl [Anne Marie Von Zuben],

175

who lost her hair three or four times in chemotherapy treatments and she was still there. She gave me a flower and, boy, that really hit me, that was a great one.

"Maybe now instead of being afraid and saying, 'Well, look how hard Terry tried and he's still got it,' people will say, 'Look at the effort he put in and he died of cancer. We're really going to have to try hard in order to beat it, try harder than we ever have before.' "

Terry Fox
November 24, 1980